# The Hidden Angels

A Novella By
Dan Peavler

Copyright 2026
Paperback ISBN: 978-1-953686-49-7
eBook ISBN: 978-1-953686-50-3
Library of Congress Control Number: 2026941601



WWW.LivingSpringsPublishers.com

**Living Springs
Publishers**

To my granddaughter Reagan. Her creativity and incredible imagination in writing about a little girl who was the only one who could see a pink planet inspired me to write this story.

THE  HIDDEN  ANGELS
WHICH  WAY  THE  WIND  BLOWS
A  REASON  FOR  EVERYTHING


A  kind  of  true  story

PROLOGUE

People have many lenses to look through when examining human experiences. The journey we travel is different in many ways, yet we all endure forces that transform us from both within and externally. We are a part of the same world, with the same universality of emotions and feelings that thread us together. We live through joy and suffering, courage, and fear, along with love and rejection. These contradictions are a part of life.

Over the years philosophers, psychologists, and spiritual leaders have discussed the hard subjects most humans consider at some point in their lives. For me, the question of why my father died when I was only two years old, leaving my mother to take care of five children alone on a farm out in the middle of nowhere, has lingered in my mind. This question has become more profound as I age and consider my own mortality. Defining humans' purpose for living, along with the meaning of life and the question of why dreadful things happen to people have all been great topics of discussion across cultures, since the beginning of time.

Everyone wants to be appreciated. No matter how trivial or insignificant the circumstance, people want to be valued. Something as seemingly inconsequential as offering a smile to a stranger can affect a person's life. Humans are empathetic and find happiness in discovering ways to make the world a better place.

I have been faced with tricky situations throughout my life and found that someone would always help. I was once told that angels look over me. The idea of angels existing in my life is very comforting.

Imagination is a universal method used by all people to form ideas and concepts that are not present to the senses. This book is a product of my imagination.

# ONE

Lansing, Michigan
October 1897

A brisk autumn wind swirled dried yellow and brown leaves throughout the main street of downtown Lansing, while sheriff Archie Moore tried his hardest to keep the harvest festival parade route safe and clear. Blowing debris amplified the danger for the huge crowd of delighted spectators watching the community spectacle that took place but once a year. Fifteen-hundred-pound horses, with their large hoofs pounding on the hard street, pulled colorful floats perilously close to the other parade participants, as well as within a few feet of the onlookers, many of them children, lining the street. The sheriff used his left hand to shield his eyes from a heavy gust of wind to glance in the direction of a lengthy line of people waiting at the hamburger stand across the loud and bustling street. Waiting in line was a man in his early twenties with a deep tanned face and curly chocolate brown hair. The fella was Bob Britton, the only child of Mary Margaret and Fredrick Britton, the owners of Pedals Bicycle Shop. Dodging the tuba player from the local high school band, the sheriff quickly walked across the road to the concession area.

"Bob, can I speak with you for a moment?" The burly sheriff moved to within an arm's length of the slightly built man. He momentarily stared at a hole in the lower part of Bob's grease-stained T-shirt.

"Yeah, sure," Bob uttered. His face flushed red as he stepped away from the concession line with the eyes of curious customers following him.

"I just have a couple questions I would like to ask you." He detected Bob's discomfort from being confronted but continued to speak with an authoritarian tone. "I understand Deputy Barney interviewed you right after the robbery of Sam's cigar shop. I just want to follow up."

"I told Barney everything I know."

"You told him you were at your bicycle shop from noon until four p.m. Did you notice a young man and his wife on the street in front of either your shop or Sam's when you arrived at work?"

"I didn't see anybody," Bob sighed, looking directly at the protruding jaw of the sheriff, wondering about the intentions of the lawman. He gave the deputy the same answer to the same question less than twenty-four hours earlier. He guardedly asked, "Do you think I had something to do with robbing Sam?"

"Oh my gosh no. Bob, I've known you your entire life. You are a very honest man and would never do such a thing." Everyone acquainted with the young mechanic considered him likeable and trustworthy. The sheriff stuck out his large, barrel chest and weakened the tenor of his voice, "I was just reading the deputy's report and noticed there were a few holes in the investigation."

Sheriff Moore felt bad that he made Bob think he was suspicious of him being a criminal. The Brittons offered a great service to the public because of their ability to repair broken machines. Yet even with their talent, the family was struggling financially, as were many other families in the city.

"I really wish I could help you sheriff. I think the person who smacked Sam on the head and stole his money was a drifter. Someone not from around here. I can't think of a person who doesn't like Sam." Bob turned his body to shield himself from a gust of wind.

"Actually, Bob, the thief didn't hit Sam on the head. His injuries were the result of losing his balance and falling backwards off a small ladder while reaching for a box on a shelf. The accident occurred before they discovered the missing items. We are still investigating just how much was stolen, but it is my understanding, now this is all according to Barney, whoever stole the cigar box only took a dollar and some change."

"That hardly sounds like a robbery," stated Bob.

"Sam's wife Bertha is the one who insists on having us investigate it as a robbery. Rumors and hearsay around town spread like wildfire. I am still looking into the particulars of the case. I told Barney if I ran across you today, I would ask if you remembered specifically seeing a man and his wife roaming around the building you share with Sam on the day of the incident."

"Well, he can put that to rest because nothing has changed from when I spoke with your deputy before; I don't recollect seeing anyone at all." He shook his head. "I'm glad whoever it was that stole from Sam wasn't vicious enough to hit him, but it kind of bothers me that a story like this could evolve into a major crime."

"That's human nature, people enjoy gossiping."

"Is that all you need?" Bob asked, looking at the tattered concession tent where the delicious smell of hamburgers and hot dogs permeated into the wind. "I would like to grab me a hot dog and get inside. I have a feeling the wind is going to start blowing harder."

"I have one more thing I would like to run by you. Do you know much about motor vehicles?"

"I am intrigued by the gasoline engine, but Pop and me haven't had an opportunity to work on one yet," Bob stated. He wondered if the sheriff might have purchased an automobile.

"There is a lot happening with the automobile business, right here in Lansing." The sheriff glanced at Bob's worn shoes. "With your abilities to repair contraptions, it seems like it would be a great opportunity for you to pursue a career in the industry."

"I haven't given it too much thought. I suppose with a little training I would be able to work on an automobile."

"An opportunity to do that might be available for you," the sheriff declared. "Eli Olds is planning on expanding the Olds Motor Vehicle Company."

"I thought he just started the company."

"He did. But there's talk about him partnering with Samuel L. Smith. If he does, then there will be a lot of money being invested here in this city."

"How is this an opportunity for me?" Bob brought his hand to his chin.

"Eli plans to have a meeting where he and his team are going to interview potential employees for the company. Getting in on the ground floor of this enterprise is something many people will be trying to be a part of." A serious look came to the sheriff's face. "I know Eli well enough that I can get you an interview."

"I'm not sure if I am qualified to work for a big company. The only place I've ever worked is in our bicycle shop." Bob looked at the sheriff's eagle eyes. His eyes were constantly moving as if they were hunting prey.

"Eli is a good person who has a knack for finding gifted individuals. When I heard they were looking for talented people, I thought about you," proclaimed Sheriff Moore. "Having a reliable paycheck might give you a chance to enjoy the small things in life."

"Thank you, Sheriff. If you can arrange an interview for me with Mr. Olds, I would really appreciate it." For just the briefest of moments Bob wondered why the sheriff was being overly supportive of him. But he knew he was stuck in life, and a change was in order.

"I'll let you know as soon as I receive more information. You have a wonderful day, Bob."

# TWO

The Pedals bicycle shop smelled of grease and cigar smoke, but every nut, bolt, and tool was positioned neatly in place, and the worn, wood plank floor was clean enough to eat off. Bob's relaxed manner of working would cause one to figure him to be lethargic. His efficiency and skill of tuning a bicycle made it all look easy. There was nary a problem that any of the cycle riding machines could pose which he could not figure out and repair. Although he and his father were both knowledgeable and effectual at working on apparatus of all kinds, their business was failing. It was a miracle they survived through the past four years of the country's terrible depression. But now, with the turn of the century quickly approaching and the inevitable acceptance of the automobile as a mode of transportation, bicycles were becoming increasingly irrelevant. The time when people enjoyed gentle rides in the countryside on a bike soon would be replaced by excursions in the comfort of an automobile.

With a flick of his wrist Bob spun the wheel of an expensive Van Cleve bicycle. The wheel rotated without even the hint of a wobble. The owner, Mr. Wilcox, was one of his father's closest and oldest friends and after checking for problems and servicing the bicycle, it was ever apparent that he was giving work to Pedals out of the goodness of his heart. Bob had helped Mr. Wilcox purchase the high-end bicycle from the Wright Cycle Shop in Dayton, Ohio. Mr. Wilcox then hired Bob to create and replace the original handlebar with one whittled down and carved from a solid piece of oak, making it one of the most unique bicycles in all of Lansing. Crafting and fitting the wooden handlebar was something Bob was immensely proud of.

Bob heard the slamming of the front door as his father and mother entered the small shop. As they approached, he could tell by the expressions on their faces that they were troubled. Mary Margaret had shoulder length blond hair and a slender figure while his father, Fredrick, was a stout man with chocolate brown hair and a dark complexion. They both stood curiously close to him without saying a word.

"What's going on, Pops?" Although he wanted to meet a girl and get married, it hadn't happened yet, and now that his grandparents had passed, the two of them were the only people in the world that he was close to. "You look like there is something serious on your mind."

"Son, I have to be honest with you," Fredrick held his clean-shaved chin high. "The shop is finished. Kaput. We have no clients and soon we won't have any food if we continue down the same dead-end road."

"I've known this was coming for a while. I wish we could make our business profitable, but

I understand we are beating a dead horse." Bob spun the wheel of the bicycle hard in defiance to show how unfair it was that someone so capable could not make a living. He was more worried about his parents than himself. He turned his attention to his dad. "Have you thought about what you will do?"

"Don't worry about us. I have lots of options." Fredrick picked up a small piece of metal from the floor and flicked it into the waste basket.

"No matter what happens, we'll survive," Bob professed. He spotted his mother's sad eyes. "Ma, I don't want you to worry about me either."

"Of course we are going to worry about you. Bob, you are an exceptionally good person, and I can't believe the world we live in wouldn't reward you."

With a frown on his face, Fredrick gazed at the few hand tools scattered on the bench. He dropped his eyes to stare blankly. Only a couple months earlier he traveled to Ohio to observe how some of the bicycle shops were using the latest technology of lathes, band saws and drill presses all powered by overhead belts connected to a gas engine. At that time, he was optimistic he would be able to modernize his shop.

"What are you thinking, Pop?"

"I am thinking how time is flying. I talked with Orville and Wilbur Wright in Dayton, and they now find themselves in the same predicament of a failing business with their bicycle stores," Fredrick spoke with a dismal tone to his voice. "All their shops are going to be closing sooner than later. Everything is happening so quickly."

"I've heard rumors about the Wright brothers wanting to create a machine that flies. One thing for sure is that they are both ambitious and smart."

"No smarter than you." Fredrick clenched his fist and shook it once. "Son, I have never in my life met anyone with the knack to figure out a problem and resolve it as easily as you do."

"It doesn't seem to be making us much money."

"It's the times we live in son. There are a lot of people like us who can't dig themselves out from under the tough times we have been experiencing."

"Some of my friends are trying to tell me that the system is rigged and there is no way we can ever succeed. I just don't believe there aren't avenues for us to flourish," Bob proclaimed.

"Sheriff Moore stopped by the house this morning, hoping to speak with you. Samuel L. Smith and Eli Olds are giving interviews to a very select group of businessmen from all around the country, not just from Lansing." Fredrick shook his fist again. "Sheriff Moore is a savior. He has secured a spot for you to interview with the group."

"The sheriff told me all of this the other day," Bob confessed. "I meant to speak with you about interviewing with these powerful men. It worries me that I might not be qualified for working on an automobile. But I sure would like to give it a shot."

"Timing is everything. This could secure your future. Set you up for life," Fredrick boldly declared. "This is more important than you can ever realize."

"It's a miracle that this opportunity would come now. We believe in you, Bob," Mary Margaret looked proudly at her son. "We need to get you some new clothes for this occasion."

"When is the interview?"

"It's the day after tomorrow."

Bob smiled at his parents. After talking with the sheriff at the festival, he couldn't get the thought of meeting with the mighty men out of his mind. The more he thought about convincing Eli Olds that he could bring many skills to his new company, the more he looked forward to the challenge. All he had to do was get in front of the businessmen and he would sell himself. "I'll do it for all three of us. I'll give it my all to get a job working for Mr. Olds.

"Yes." Fredrick shook his fist. "That's my boy."

"I'll ride Mr. Wilcox's bicycle out to him tomorrow." He stared at his parents with his heart beating rapidly against his chest. His greatest fear was to disappoint them. "Walking back from the Wilcox farm will give me a chance to think of what I can say in the interview."

# THREE

Bob used his strong legs to pedal the bicycle down a narrow gravel road in the direction of the Wilcox farm. The weather could change at any time, but this day was sunny and glorious, with only a few clouds in the sky. He leaned back on the seat and allowed the almost leafless trees to fly by as he traveled through the wide-open countryside with the clean, cool air flowing o'er his face. The beautiful fall colors were nearly gone, bringing about a deep sense of change. Cresting over a steep hill, he noticed a hand pulled wagon on the side of the road at the bottom of the knoll.

A middle-aged man crouched down, laboring on the wheel of the wagon while a woman and two young girls watched him work. The two girls, both with disheveled hair, wore heavy wool socks with no shoes. A tattered blanket hung from each of their shoulders. The man glanced up when Bob stopped only a couple feet from where he was working. The woman, dressed in an oversized, torn jacket with the stuffing visible on the right sleeve, moved closer to the children and placed her arms out, shielding them from the stranger.

"Can I give you a hand?" Bob inquired, straddling his bike. He noticed the man's hands were covered in grease.

"We're good." The man glanced up at him. He had a thin face and a crooked nose. "Nothing major, the wheel was just beginning to squeak."

"It was wobbling and getting harder to pull," the woman specified in a very calm voice.

Bob leaned the bike onto the back side of the wagon. He bent down to take a better look. The man seemed uneasy with him standing over his shoulder.

"My name's Bob Britton." Bob stepped back and smiled at the two girls. Both were a spitting image of their father with large ears and oblong noses.

"Tony Mickelson." The man rose from the wheel. He held up his greasy hand and motioned in the direction of his family. "My wife Barbara, Beth Ann, and Britney."

"I'm taking this bicycle to the next farmhouse less than two miles ahead." Bob pointed down the road. "If you stop there, we can put the wagon up on blocks and I'll help you fix it properly."

The man looked at his wife. She nodded.

"Alright. We'll meet you there," he replied, wiping his hands on a very dirty rag.

As fate would have it, the Wilcox were not home. This meant that Bob would have to leave the bicycle in their garage without obtaining payment for his services. In a way it was karma that he wasn't going to receive money for repairs that were not needed in the first place. He knew the old couple would have no problem with him borrowing tools and using a jack to lift the hand cart so he could help repair the wheel for the traveling family.

Bob waited patiently as he watched Tony, with his wife walking by his side, pull the heavy wagon down the short driveway from the main road to the farm. The tops of the two girls' heads, riding in the back of the cart, were barely visible. He motioned for the man to pull the rickety wagon next to the shop.

"I'll pull the wheel off and pack the hub," Bob stressed confidently.

"Here, I can climb under and set the jack." Tony was on his back shimmying under the wagon before Bob could reply.

"Thank you so much for this help. All we need to do is have this old wagon stay together long enough to get to Potterville," Barbara declared.

"Is that where you live?" Bob moved back from the wagon to stand next to Barbara while Tony pumped the jack to lift the wheel off the ground.

"No, it's where my aunt lives. Aunt Becca is sick and wants us to come and help her. Since I am expecting another one," she spoke with a tranquil voice, holding her hand on her belly, "I imagine she will help us as much as we help her."

"Have you been on the road long?"

"It seems like forever since we left Alpena."

The two men worked quickly to pull the wagon wheel and repair the hub. It was quite a simple job for Bob, and when they finished the work he was confident the wheel would be reliable to get the family to Potterville.

"We really appreciate what you have done for us. I wish there was some way I could repay you," said Tony.

"Thank you so much," added Barbara. "You wouldn't believe the amount of bad luck we have had over the past month."

"No payment needed," Bob stated firmly, leaning an arm on the back of the wagon. "I know if the Wilcox were here, they would have made sure to have fed us too."

Bob glanced into the back of the wagon. Laying on top of one of the blankets was a "Firebrand" newspaper. Sitting right next to the tabloid was a box for cigars that had a sticker from Sam's cigar shop on the top corner. He stared sharply at Tony, who instantly recognized that Bob had discovered the stolen property. Bob moved away from the wagon.

"Tony, can I speak with you for a moment?" Bob picked up the jack and stepped inside the entrance of the small shop building.

"Sure." Tony glanced at his family before following Bob into the structure.

"Ok, listen," Bob said in a low, but intense voice. "I am going to ask you man to man. Did you steal that cigar box from Sam's cigar shop?"

"I took it." Tony could see that Bob was infuriated. He held his hands out and put his palms together as if he were praying. "Please hear me out. I'm a very honest and moral man. Please let me tell you what happened."

"Ok, convince me, because I'm about ready to haul you back to town and turn you over to the sheriff."

"My family and I arrived in Lansing without a penny to our name. We were all very hungry. I left Barbara and the girls at a park to see if I could find work. I went into Sam's cigar shop to inquire if he had any chores. I told him I would work for either food or money. Sam's a very good man who told me I could clean up around the back of the shop for a payment of one dollar and twenty-five cents. I worked nonstop from eight that morning until about four in the afternoon, most of the time outside cleaning the shed at the back of the building. When I finished, I walked through the back door of the store to the front, but there was nobody around. The shop is not very big, and I realized immediately Sam wasn't there. The front door was locked and the closed sign posted in the window. The cigar box you saw in the wagon was sitting on the counter next to the cash machine and there was one dollar and three pennies on top of it. I took the box and the money." Tony stared at Bob for a moment, noticing he was patiently listening, so he continued. "I planned on going back and confirming with Sam, to make sure he was ok with me taking the money and cigar box for payment. But after picking up Barbara and the girls, we stopped at the grocery store to get some food. I heard people talking about Sam being assaulted and robbed. They were all terribly angry, alleging that he was on his death bed after nearly being murdered, so I thought the best course for me and my family was to leave town as fast as we could."

Bob could see outside the door where Barbara and her daughters were waiting in the cool breeze. He turned and looked directly at Tony, and said, "Ok, you told me you are a moral man. I believe you know the difference between right and wrong."

"Thank you, I do know the difference." Tony waited for Bob to resume.

"The reason Sam wasn't in the shop was because he fell and injured himself. His wife Bertha is the one who called the sheriff and made the claim of robbery."

"Under different circumstances I would have returned to the shop and cleared everything up with Sam. Bob, the people in the grocery store were so mad that I believe they would have hanged me first and asked questions later."

"Ok, but what about the newspaper? I know Firebrand is a newspaper that supports anarchist viewpoints. Are you an anarchist?" Bob inquired.

"No, no, I am not," he adamantly avowed. "The paper was given to me by a fella named

Leon who traveled with us for a while when we left Alpena. He held views on our country that I don't support. We parted ways right after I went to work at Sam's cigar shop."

"You go with your family." Bob held his hand out.

Tony grasped his hand and pulled him in for a hug.

"Thank you. You were God sent."

Bob was happy with his decision to allow Tony to go free. It would have been difficult for the poor man to receive a fair judgement if he were to return to Lansing.

A frigid wind was beginning to blow, and the weather was quickly changing for the worse. It was time for everyone to forget about the incident and be on their way. There was a lot to think about as he began the walk home.

# FOUR

It was a dank and dark morning as Bob prepared to leave for the much-anticipated interview with the executives from the Olds Motor Company. After locking the front door to the bicycle shop, he glanced into the large picture window at the front of the cigar store where Bertha and Sam were standing near the counter, partaking in an animated discussion. Sam noticed him peering through the window and immediately waved for him to come inside. A bell on the front door rang as he stepped out of the blustery weather and into the warmth.

"You sure look all fancy Bob. What are you dressed up for?" Sam asked enthusiastically.

"I'm meeting with Eli Olds people today to see about working for them." He stared at Sam's dark face with leathery bags under his eyes and a blaze of white hair over his temples.

"Good for you, Bob. That sure is a mighty powerful man for you to be rubbing shoulders with," Sam decreed.

"That would be a very good job for you to land," declared Bertha. She was short with a full, pear-shaped body and heavy brown eyebrows.

"I'm glad to see you are feeling better after falling and hitting your head," Bob offered graciously. He enjoyed the smell of fresh tobacco filling the air. The shop itself was a delight to the eyes with fancy wooden shelves and bright, colorful pictures adorning the walls.

"Yes, I feel much better. I recuperate fast."

"I think he was a warrior of some sort in a previous life," stated Bertha.

"Well Sam, I am glad to see you are doing so well now," acknowledged Bob.

"What an ordeal this has been. To be robbed on top of having Sam injured is too much," uttered Bertha angrily. "Plus, I think Deputy Barney has mishandled the entire investigation."

"The person who stole from you didn't hit Sam, did they?" Bob was surprised at Bertha's fury.

"No, but the more we checked, the more we have found was stolen from us," proclaimed Bertha. "At first I thought he took only the money out of the cash register and a box of cigars, but this morning we noticed the thief also took Sam's solid silver belt buckle he won at the state fair boxing competition nearly thirty years ago."

Bob felt his heart skip a beat. He silently stared at the couple, feeling somewhat traitorous for not immediately mentioning his interaction with Tony and his family.

"Whoever took the buckle will have a heck of a time trying to sell it because it has my name on it. There just aren't very many Sam Marciellos in the world, and only one who won the state fair middle weight boxing title in 1869," Sam proudly indicated.

"I think it was that Tony fella we hired to clean up around here, but Sam doesn't think so," lamented Bertha. "And that darn Barney went around telling everyone the thief only stole a cigar box and some pennies. He spoke before even really knowing or investigating a darn thing. I can't believe what this world has become."

"That Tony fella I hired was a very nice family man," stressed Sam sternly. "Besides when he first came up to ask about work there was another fella named Leon waiting close by. If you ask me, I think it was that man who stole our money and my buckle."

"I still think it was the guy you hired," argued Bertha, flinching her eyebrows, "if it wasn't him then he was an accomplice in the crime. None of them seemed like very righteous people to me."

"How much money was taken?" Bob asked gloomily, hoping it wasn't more than a dollar and a few pennies.

"There was eight or nine dollars in the cash register, and we had close to forty dollars in the cash box that was hidden under the counter with the silver belt buckle." Bertha rolled her eyes. "We should never have had that belt buckle anywhere near the shop, but old bigshot Sam here liked to show it off to the customers."

"Sam, I'm glad you are doing better. I must get going to my interview," Bob declared, using a conciliatory tone.

He pulled the collar of his sportscoat tight around his neck as he walked briskly in the direction of downtown. He suffered another moment of guilt for not telling Sam and Bertha about his encounter with helping Tony fix his wagon. He still believed the man to be moral, knowing that there must be more to what happened with the robbery of Sam. The remorse was short lived because his thought moved to the importance of the interview.

***

With chestnut brown oak paneling and a huge chandelier hanging from a fifteen-foot-high ceiling, the room for the meeting was far fancier than Bob could have imagined. Although he dressed in the finest clothes he had ever worn, he was still underdressed. Two men in black suits stood at a podium in front of two rows of ten chairs. Every person in the room was conversing with someone else, except for him. He stood awkwardly alone, listening in the shadows to their stories of conquest and betrayal. For a man who had always made an honest living with his hands, he felt uneasy in a room filled with ambitious men rich with duplicity. He held a strong feeling of not belonging.

"Everyone, please find a seat." The loud voice coming from the tallest of the men at the front of the room rang off the solid wood paneling. Having the meeting started was a great relief for

Bob. He moved to the center of the back row and fell into a chair.

"Listen closely, everyone. Mr. Olds and Mr. Smith are about to arrive at the Palmer House just down the street," the tall man stated. "These two men are very busy. As soon as they are ready to address you, we will walk, as a group, down to the Palmer House. They will select those of you who they want to further continue in this process."

"Will we be able to pose our own questions to Mr. Olds?" asked a distinguished older gentleman with graying hair, sitting in the front row.

"No, Michael, not to them. They have a good understanding of your qualifications. They will be the ones asking questions. You can ask us anything you would like."

Bob shuffled in his seat. He was sitting on a cushioned folding chair, shoulder to shoulder with two middle-aged men wearing very fancy suits. The smell of sweetness from their cologne filled his nostrils. A moment of dread entered his mind, wondering if his entire being was at the whim of fate.

"There is a rumor that Olds Motor Vehicle Company is going to relocate out of Lansing," A man from the front row spoke with confidence. "Is that true?"

"I'll let Bartholomew answer that question." The tall man stepped back and allowed a man with jet black hair parted directly down the center of his head to stand at the podium.

"There is nothing set in stone for anything concerning the future of this company moving from Michigan," he spoke quickly. "The rumors you have been hearing are just that: rumors."

"How many people are they looking for in management?" A man in the front row asked.

"To start out with, it could be only a couple of you." The man at the podium slowed his cadence as he spoke, making his statement seem more believable. "Eventually it could be all of you."

"Can I ask you a question?" Bob rose from his chair.

"Of course you can Bob, shoot away."

Bob's jaw dropped from the surprise of the powerful man in the suit recognizing him by name. "I am wondering if it is only management people you are hiring," he stammered slightly. "I'm a mechanic and wonder if I might be in the wrong place."

The front door behind him opened, allowing a cold wind to enter the room. A man walked quickly along the side of the chairs in the direction of the podium.

"We know all about you, Bob. We plan to hire capable and competent people, period. You have as good a chance of finding a job as anyone here." The interviewer gave him a confident nod.

Wetness covered the head of the man who just entered the room. He scurried to the podium and stepped in front of the two men. He yelled, "Everyone, listen up, we need to hurry. Mr. Olds and Mr. Smith have arrived at the Palmer House and are waiting. They are very, very busy and we must hurry."

Bob hesitated for a moment, hearing the clatter of chairs as everyone else quickly rose. He felt much better about his chances of having a fair shot at working for the large company. Making enough money to afford his family some dignity was now in reach. All the men rushed to the door. By the time he arrived at the exit from the conference room, he was last in line to leave.

It was bitterly cold outside, and now an icy sleet fell from the dark sky. The men in front of him jogged in the direction of the Palmer House, which was two hundred yards away, with their expensive shoes splashing water as they maneuvered through shallow puddles of slush, most of them covered with an umbrella. He shielded his face from the frozen rain and trotted behind the group of businessmen. Approaching the stairs going up to the entrance of the decorative stone building he noticed each of the men in front of him hesitate momentarily, staring off to the right, before scampering up the steps and rushing through the door. When he came closer, he could see an elderly lady lying on the wet ground with a small boy hovering over her.

"Help me, please," the old lady pleaded with a bright blue shawl hanging loosely across her shoulders. She was holding her leg as wetness covered her gray hair. There was a small puddle of blood blending with the water on the road below her.

"Please, mister, please help us. My granny is hurt," the little boy yelled as he nestled over the lady, protecting his grandmother the best he could from the sleet, with water dripping from his flushed face. His large brown eyes were fully opened in fear.

Every cell in Bob's brain told him to keep going to the interview, but every fiber from his soul told him to help the elderly woman. He made the choice to stop and help.

"Can you stand?" he asked, falling to a knee by her side. She stared back at him through fading blue eyes with a grimace on her face. There was a large laceration on the lower part of her leg.

"No, I can't get up. Something blew off the building up there and hit my leg. I think it is broken." She was struggling to breathe. She closed her eyes.

Bob glanced at the construction area full of building materials perilously perched high up on the steep roof of a large, red brick building. He turned his attention to the small boy who was about eight years old.

"You need to run and get help," Bob said firmly to the little boy.

The youngster looked back with a blank expression.

"What's your name?" Bob asked.

"Everyone calls me Smithy."

"Ok, Smithy, do you know where the hardware store is on main street? It is only about five blocks away."

"I know where it is." He vigorously shook his head in affirmation with droplets of water falling to the brick street.

"Go and tell Mr. Wilburn that your grandma is hurt, and that we need an ambulance."

The little boy took off in full sprint with his feet splashing water behind him.

Bob hunched over the lady and shielded her from the ice pellets falling from the sky. The back of the new jacket his mother bought him for the interview was quickly becoming a coat of ice.

"You are God sent," the lady stated with a barely conscious voice as she slumped further down to rest her head on the brick street.

"Please rest. Help will be here shortly."

Bob felt the cold moisture on the back of his neck trickle down his spine underneath his jacket, soaking his shirt. He wished that he could move the lady from the wet, icy road but all he could do was protect her. The piercing pain of the cold, frozen rain hitting the back of his neck, freezing the nerves in his spine, was almost unbearable, but he continued to shield her until he heard the stomping of horse hoofs hitting the hard street, a welcoming sound of the approaching ambulance. He rose above the semi-conscious woman with the ice on his coat breaking away. The back side of his pants were soaked.

"You did good Bob," Sheriff Moore dressed in full rain gear placed a hand on his shoulder, "you need to go inside and dry off."

Bob watched silently as the rescue team lifted the lady onto a stretcher. Approaching the stairs to the Palmer House, he heard the faint voice of the small boy yell, "thank you, mister."

He staggered up the steps to the impressive hand carved wood door, where just inside the interviews were being held. It was locked. He pounded hard, but no answer. He continued to hammer on the door for a full thirty seconds. It partially opened, only enough for the man inside to peek out.

"I am one of the people who is here to interview with Mr. Olds. They are expecting me," Bob pleaded. The face of the person inside the sliver of a door was a faceless dark silhouette.

"Go away, lad." The man spoke firmly with an Irish accent.

"But I need this interview," He gasped in a weak voice. The warm air flowing from the opening of the door momentarily gave him relief from the shivering cold. Water dripped from his soaked locks.

"Go home son, there is no way I will allow you in here looking like you do. They have already broken out the liquid refreshments. You missed your opportunity." The man slammed the door closed.

"But I..." Bob turned and walked down the icy stairs with his head hanging low.

He was soaked from head to toe whilst he hesitated at the spot where only moments earlier the little, old lady lay in pain. A slight rumbling sound from above caused him to look up. The last thing he saw was the end of a twenty-foot two-by-twelve wood plank falling from the construction site on the roof overhead. It hit him square on his forehead with a loud thump.

# FIVE

A blinding, bright, white light triggered Bob to slam his eyes shut. When he opened them, he was sitting on a bench in front of a crystal-clear river running through a park of bright green lawns and trees. The sky above was a perfect Cerulean blue.

"What in the hell just happened!" he yelled, leaning back on the hard bench.

"Watch your language," shouted a lady with a slow, gravelly voice, sitting only a foot away, keenly staring at him, with her arms crossed. "Now take a deep breath and release it."

"What happened?"

"Just relax." Her face was wrinkled and her voice sounded as though she had just smoked a carton of cigarettes. "It's going to take a moment before you recollect everything."

"I remember getting hit in the head with a piece of lumber. Does my father know where I am?"

"Not those memories," her rough voice was remarkably calming. "Lean back and rest for a bit."

Bob propped his head back; his mind was still foggy. The sounds of the wind blowing through the trees and birds singing prompted a recollection of the beautiful park.

"I have been here before. Haven't I?" He turned to look at the lady.

"Yes, you have." She was smiling.

"I'm dead, ain't I?"

"Dead as a door nail," she confirmed, emphasizing each word.

"And you're here to help me transition?"

"Yes I am."

"I'm worried about how my mother and father are going to take it with me being gone." He hesitated for a moment. "I miss them."

"Those emotions will go away very quickly," her raspy voice was nearly a whisper. "Everyone you left behind is just fine."

"Everything is ok, Bobby." The fluorescent image of an old man standing in the distance spoke with an animated tone.

"Grandpa."

"Yes Bobby," he stated excitedly, "we'll talk soon." He disappeared.

"What happens now?" Bob pulled his shirt away from his chest and looked down. He had never seen the clothes he was wearing before.

"Reach into the breast pocket of your shirt and take out the card."

He pulled out a three-by-three postcard with four numbers, one in each corner.

"Wow, you are getting quite an upgrade."

He stared at her dumfounded.

"The number fourteen, in the left-hand corner is your previous level, and the number 24 is what you have progressed to." She raised her eyebrows and nodded downward. "That is an almost unheard-of rise in status. You have impressed someone."

"What about the other two?"

"Do not worry about those two, they are location numbers. I'm here to help you with them," she proudly announced.

Off in the distance he could see a tall grayish blue building rising into the blue sky that seemed to travel forever into the distance. Although his thoughts were cloudy, the sight of the large building boosted his memory as to the process he was about to experience. The lady looked at him with a proud look on her face.

"We can go anytime you are ready. They are all waiting." She held her hand on her chest as she tried to stifle a cough.

"How long is this going to take?"

"Time is an earthly concept." She cleared her throat.

"Of course, I remember. Are you an angel?" He could tell immediately by the slanted look she gave him that he had hit a nerve with her.

"Don't you worry about who I am," she said with a huff, clearing her throat again. "My job is to make you feel comfortable. To give you both a sense of clarity and a sense of blessedness as we move through this process."

"I'm ready to go."

"It won't be long before you recall everything."

Within a blink of an eye, they were inside a massive room with walls of different pastel colors. Sitting behind a desk of pure, clear glass was a lady with a perfect, welcoming smile. Her presence was that of someone very old, but her face had a brightness shining from around it without a sign of a wrinkle.

"Come in. Please come in and take a seat." She motioned to a padded leather chair to the side of her desk. "I have finished refreshing myself on your past."

"I recall some of this."

"There are decisions you need to make." She looked at him tenderly but with some intensity.

"I'm remembering."

She smiled at him. "The choices you make here about the importance you place on family, fame, wealth, and other aspects of life on Earth will greatly increase the probability of you accomplishing them."

"Is my life on Earth predetermined?"

"No. You are free to make choices that will determine your own meaning and purpose."

"I have angels watching over me, don't I?"

"Yes, you have angels that watch over you."

"I remember much of this." He felt a sense of euphoria that brought him much comfort. "I have a question."

"Questions are good, but they will be answered in the manner as to how you ask them."

"Do my angels help me succeed on Earth?"

"Yes."

"How do they help me?"

"Not in any specific way. They are caretakers of hope and possibilities that you request. They have methods to guide you away from fear, toward abundance and all the amazing things available for you that often go unnoticed. They don't make decisions for you; they help you realize your dreams in very inconspicuous ways, pushing you in the direction of righteousness and, ultimately, happiness. That is why it is important for them to know what you desire in life."

"Why can't I remember all of this when I'm on Earth?"

"You sense that there is more, but if you knew without doubt that you were coming here after you died, it would alter how you lived on Earth. Everything that makes life worth living would be lost," her voice was soothing. "Do you have any more questions? Now is the time to ask about anything."

"I saw my grandfather when I first arrived. Will I be able to speak with my grandparents?"

"You are going to feel the essence of them when you go through that door behind you."

He turned and looked at the tall door with a bright light radiating from the threshold.

"You should never be afraid to ask for things. You won't always receive them, but it doesn't hurt to ask."

"I really can't think of anything now." He had a feeling he should be asking for more information. "Wait, I do have a question. Why did I die so young?"

"Free will is both a part of your material as well as spiritual being. People who die doing something honorable are looked upon very highly, but it is not the reason you died."

"So, you judge my actions on Earth?"

"Of course we do. We certainly are not going to help people do bad things to others."

"How am I rewarded for being moral?"

"You gain more angels." The sparkle from her face expressed to him that she was pleased with his presence. "Is there anything else?"

"Can I pick my name for when I go back?"

"Go ahead."

"Henry."

"That's a strong name."

"I am ready to meet my angels."

"Everyone you want to speak with is behind that door."

The door opened to a blue sky of sparkling diamonds. He closed his eyes. He didn't need to see them; he could feel the presence of his angels all around. Peacefulness and pure bliss.

# SIX

Mürringen, Belgium
December 1944

Henry Dewey sat on a metal bucket in front of a slow burning fireplace in the living area of a stone farmhouse located on the northeastern edge of Mürringen, Belgium, a small Ardennes village near the German border. Snowflakes spit from low hanging clouds, creating a cold and blustery scene outside, while he huddled on a stone floor with five members of the 371st Field Artillery, Battery C, 99th Infantry. Each time he moved away from the fireplace, the bitter cold helped him realize that being quartered in the farmhouse was a blessing. He and his fellow soldiers were luckier than the members of the infantry scattered throughout the Ardennes Forest who endured the freezing nights in fox holes.

Henry and most of the soldiers in his outfit were happy to simply follow orders and do their small part to fight the evil Nazi regime that was attempting to take over the world. So far, the only combat they experienced, besides reports of a few sniper attacks, was that of fighting the cold. The rumor was that the war could be over by the first of the year. They had rushed across France only a month earlier, but already the hope was that their visit would be short lived and everyone would be heading back home right after Christmas. While sharing a bottle of cognac found in the small cellar of the farmhouse, the conversation on that Friday night was the same for all five soldiers; it was anticipation in finding a nice girl to marry and starting a family when they returned to the states.

"I know this may sound stupid," stated Private Smith after taking a big swig from the bottle of cognac, "but we should all take in the moments we share here and relish every adventure. It's something we can tell our kids."

"You're right, Smithy, it does sound stupid," countered Private Thornburg, mockingly.

"I just received a letter from my girl, Beth Ann, back home," interjected Private Barnes. "She says all the newspapers are saying the war should be over real soon."

"My mother's name is Beth Ann," proclaimed Smithy, staring at the greenish glass of the bottle in his hand.

"The name of my girl has nothing to do with what I am telling you guys. We might be going home before we even fire a shot. Now pass the bottle to someone else."

"Names are important. Everybody called my grandpa Smithy, and then my daddy Smithy, and now everyone calls me Smithy." He leaned to hand the bottle to Henry.

"Ok, Smithy, I'm not going to argue with you, names are important," said private Barnes annoyingly.

"When I get back to Texas, I'm going to find me a good woman and get married. I plan on finding some acreage and build my own home," declared Private Tom Baker with a southern drawl.

"I already built my house back home in Michigan." Smithy felt the warmth of the liquor burning in his belly.

"Of course you did. You always need be a step better than everyone, don't you, Smithy?" Private Baker shook his head.

"Well, I did build a house." Smithy looked directly at Henry. "Didn't I, Henry?"

"I don't know if you did or not Smithy, but since you said you did, I believe you." Henry's empathetic manner came naturally. He was a handsome man, six feet tall, with dark curly hair and deep dark eyes on a chiseled face. Whereas Smithy's face was oblong with pointy ears and a large, crooked nose, who slumped over to the point of being a hunchback. His odd appearance caused him to have a life of bullying and hounding. From the time they met at training camp, Henry was constantly having to help the awkward private. He, along with most of the other soldiers, experienced tough times growing up during the Depression era, and few of them had more than a seventh-grade education. It was eleven o'clock when the group decided to go to bed in the loft.

Five miles to the south of where Henry and his fellow soldiers laid their heads down for the night, thousands of troops from Germany's 6th Panzer Army, commanded by SS Obertrgruppenfuhrer Sepp Dietrich, waited to pounce on them in a surprise attack. Adolf Hitler gave Dietrich's Panzer Army priority for supplies and equipment in the well thought out plan to split the allied forces by moving to Antwerp through the northern point of Belgium. Conditions were perfect, with cloud cover eliminating the American air superiority. The attack was scheduled to start at 5:30 in the morning.

A loud thud woke Henry, followed by a deafening explosion. A shell smashed through the stone wall of the barn connected to the house he was sleeping in and exploded in a small haystack. He jumped from his sleeping area and pulled on his boots. The piercing voice of Sergeant Steven Mathews ordered everyone out of the house. Explosions from enemy shells caused chaos as everyone ran out the front door in the direction of a large field that housed the artillery guns. The sound of deadly shrapnel striking the buildings and trees after each explosion was earsplitting. The barrage of shells being bombarded on their location made it difficult to assemble the guns to fire back at the enemy in support of the forward troops. None the less, the deafening sound of the 371st own artillery guns soon filled the air. They fired until they were finally out of ammunition.

Everyone was ordered to grab their rifles and prepare to fight.

"Smithy, we need to start all the trucks," Henry yelled to his friend, who remained right on his shoulder through the initial attack, with his breath visible in the extreme cold. The dirty air stung his nostrils, and the smoke blurred his vision. "There isn't any chance we can stay here for very long."

A dense fog mixed with the smoke made visibility to be less than a quarter mile. Smithy glanced southward in the direction of the forest where the sound of rapid gunfire could be heard. He couldn't see through the trees, but he knew major fighting was occurring very close to them and getting closer.

"Henry, we need to get out of here," Smithy yelled, pointing his M1 Garand service rifle into the fog. The heavy smell of smoke was becoming worse to the point of being unbearable.

Henry started the truck before hopping out of the cab, grabbing his rifle, and moving to the next truck. Smithy followed right behind.

"Henry, the Germans are right there." Smithy pointed to the south. "We need to go."

Henry started another truck and jumped from the cab. He placed a hand on Smithy's shoulder and looked him directly in the eyes. "We can't leave until we get orders to move. I'm sure we will get them soon, but until we do you need to help me start the trucks."

"We just received orders from the brass to move back toward Elsenborn Ridge," yelled Sergeant Mathews. "Hook the artillery guns and let's get out of here."

Henry tossed his rifle onto the front seat of the closest truck and jumped into the driver's seat. Smithy hopped in right next to him. Henry spun the tires as he backed up to one of the artillery guns. It only took a moment to attach the weaponry to the trucks and be on the road. The sound of enemy gunfire was close behind.

They drove a little over a mile down a narrow road before they came upon a tank stuck in front of a bridge. It was impossible for them to bypass the tank. A decision was quickly made to abandon the vehicles and artillery guns. They would have to move forward on foot.

"We need to drain the gas from these trucks and disable the guns," Corporal Jones yelled as he ran from truck to truck. "We received information that English speaking German soldiers have been caught in the area dressed as American soldiers. Don't trust anyone."

Smithy perched his gun on the hood of the truck and aimed to the south, protecting his friend, as Henry worked on draining the gasoline. Small explosions occurred in unison as the artillery was disabled. Everyone began to trot across the bridge through the darkness in the direction of the little town of Krinkelt.

Jogging shoulder to shoulder with Henry, through the snow, Smithy declared, in a low voice, "This is a time where we don't want to be first."

"I agree with you on that. I have a feeling there are a lot more Germans than we are thinking."

"I just want to tell you that I have been very lucky to have you as my friend. You are a good man, Henry." Smithy was breathing heavily. "If something happens to me, I hope you make it home and have a great life."

"Stop with that, Smithy. We need to concentrate. Keep an eye out for the enemy." Henry felt a great sense of apprehension about his friend worrying so much about him.

By the time they reached a hill overlooking Krinkelt it was past midnight. A major battle was raging in the town with much of it on fire. The flash of tracer shells from tanks firing at each other and the sound of explosions made the chaotic scene seem surreal.

"We have orders to continue forward to Sourbrodt," yelled Corporal Jones.

Tired and cold, Henry trudged ahead through the dark, following the other members of his unit, with Smithy right by his side. It became eerily quiet as they slipped down a hill to a flat area near a grove of trees. They heard voices ahead. Everyone stopped and went to their knees on the snow-covered ground.

"Who are you with?" a voice screamed from the blackness in the trees.

"371st," yelled Lieutenant Jeffrey, leaning down with his right knee sunk into deep snow.

"Come on forward."

"Who are you with?" The lieutenant asked skeptically. He waited for a moment and asked again, "who are you with?"

"3rd Platoon Observation."

"If you are an observation platoon, why are you so far north?" asked the lieutenant.

"The damn Germans chased us out."

Lieutenant Jeffrey looked back at the troops and shook his head. He motioned with his hand for everyone to lay flat onto the snow-covered field. Smithy stood up and pointed his rifle at the trees.

Flashes from the German weapons filled the darkness as three bullets hit Smithy. All soldiers from the 371st leveled their rifles and returned fire. The battle was over in minutes.

Henry was immediately at Smithy's side. He was still conscious and breathing. Blood was coming out of his nose.

"Dammit Smithy, why did you stand up?" Henry placed a hand on his shoulder. There was no doubt his friend was mortally wounded.

"Just wanted to protect you guys," he said weakly.

Smithy made a gurgling sound, smiled, took two more breaths, and died.

After Smithy's death, the war passed quickly for Henry. Many of his friends became casualties, but he continued to fight. The 371st supplied support as members of the 99th Infantry crossed the Rhine River over Ludendorff Bridge. When the Americans and their allies acquired a foothold inside the border of Germany, it was the beginning of the end of the war. They moved deeper into the Rhur pocket in the center of Germany. The unthinkable atrocities of concentration camps became visible and known to the soldiers, justifying why they were called to Europe to fight.

Henry wrote notes about all the major events in a small, black notebook he kept in his shirt pocket. He wanted to honor the loss of Smithy by remaining mindful of all he witnessed. He hoped and prayed the completion of the war was near. When the 99th Infantry attached to the 3rd Army led by General George Patton, a great sense of pride for all they accomplished was finally realized. They moved toward Bavaria with little resistance from the decimated German Army. After crossing the Danube River, news spread that the Germans had surrendered. He was going home.

# SEVEN

The nightmare of war was over. When Henry arrived back home in Joplin, Missouri, he was greeted with some joy from his family, but otherwise little fanfare. He stayed in a shed behind his mother's home and worked at menial jobs, saving enough money to buy an old pickup truck. When summer arrived, he became antsy. The harvest of wheat was in full swing across the Great Plains, and he planned to make his way west to central Kansas where his farming skills would be in high demand.

Henry left Joplin early in the morning and by early afternoon pulled into a café in Hays, Kansas. The smell of bacon and fresh bread greeted him as he sat on a round stool at the counter of a clean coffee shop, noticing several patrons sitting in leather booths scattered around the establishment. A man sitting three stools down, blatantly staring at him, was much more noticeable than the rest.

"Hello, amigo," the man spoke with a thick accent. "You have just come from the war, no?"

"Yes." Henry lowered his eyes and cocked his head away from the man. "I did fight in the war," he whispered.

"I thank you for doing so." The man quickly moved to the stool right next to Henry. "I see you do not want to talk about it, but it is finished, and now it is the time for you to live a good life. You should enjoy every moment you have on this beautiful Earth we live on."

Henry nodded slightly but didn't speak.

"I can tell you are looking for work." The man moved his face uncomfortably close to Henry's.

"What makes you think that?" Henry asked surprisingly, turning his body in the direction of the man.

"Oh, I am very sensitive to people's needs, almost to the point of being clairvoyant," the man proclaimed lightheartedly. "That, and I saw all the tools in the bed of your pickup."

"I think you are more observant than you are psychic," Henry said, smiling at the man.

"You are probably right." The man moved back a smidgen and held out his hand. "My name is Manuel Frederico Maes."

"Henry Dewey," he shook Manuel's hand.

"But I am right, no? You are looking for work."

"You are not wrong about that."

"I know of a farmer named John Harvey who lives about two hours from here. He is hiring hands to help with harvesting wheat. I think he might be a good fit for you. In fact, the whole family might be good for you." Manuel pulled out a scrap of paper from a shirt pocket and began drawing a map. He handed it to Henry. "Follow this map to the field where you will see a large stone statue. The harvest of wheat has already started, and if you leave now, you will have plenty of time to speak with him today."

Henry stared at the piece of paper. After all the time he spent in the Army fighting to stay alive, and seeing the worst in humanity, he was overtaken by the kindness of the stranger. "Thank you," he whispered.

"Don't worry, amigo." Manuel slapped him on the back, noticing the emotions. "You should get going. Good things are in store for you."

***

Driving fast was a curse Henry carried back with him from his time fighting in Europe. He pushed the accelerator to the floorboard as he drove down a dusty, backcountry road in central Kansas. Golden waves of wheat blowing in the breeze were all you could see for miles on both sides of the road. The hot sun was still beating down from the cloudless sky when he arrived at the entrance to a partially cut wheat field marked with a large stone pillar.

He drove his pickup truck across the short stubble, until he was next to a combine where he could see the rear end of a man in bib overalls working on the straw spreader. Dust rising in the air from two other combines cutting the large wheat field was visible in the distance.

"Hello sir, can you tell me where I might find John Harvey?" Henry leaned in as close to the man as he could without hitting his head on the back of the combine.

"I'm John. How can I help you?" He pulled his head from under the machine and looked at Henry. The man's face was deep brown, and he was very tall with long hanging arms.

"I'm looking for a job." Henry noticed beads of sweat on his forehead.

"Can you drive a combine?" the farmer spoke very slowly, but firmly.

"I've been a farmhand for all my life. Anyway, that was before the war." Henry hesitated for a moment. "But I'll be honest sir, I have never driven a self-propelled combine."

"Not very many people have driven this machine." Mr. Harvey wiped his brow with a rag. "This is the Massey Harris model 21. It was almost impossible to get your hands on this combine during the war."

"I learn really fast when it comes to machinery." Henry felt comfortable with the demeanor of John Harvey, who he figured to be in his mid-thirties. Both men turned their heads to look at a truck approaching in a cloud of dust. A bright red Ford grain truck stopped about ten feet from them with steam flowing skyward from under the hood.

"The damn thing is overheating again," a woman yelled out the window. She opened the door and jumped to the ground. She pulled a ballcap from her head and shook her long red hair. She wore a button-down shirt that was a couple of sizes too large for her with the front tied at her belly button. The full curves of her body were very apparent under baggy clothes.

Henry locked eyes with her. His breathing became shallow. He was unable to pull his gaze away, something detected by Mr. Harvey.

"This is my little sister, Betty," said the older man, noticing she seemed as stricken with the handsome stranger as he was with her.

"Hi," Henry said awkwardly, unsure if he ought to offer her his hand.

"Hello," Betty said in a whisper, shifting her eyes to the side and upward without moving her head.

"Let's take a peek under the hood." Mr. Harvey grinned at the uneasiness of his sister as he stepped in the direction of the wheat truck.

"Do you mind if I have a look? I oversaw maintaining a whole fleet of trucks during the war."

"Have at it." John stepped back.

Henry perceived the levity between the older man and his sister. He was very much in his element as he opened the hood and climbed up to inspect the engine.

"It's just a hose." He proudly looked down at Betty. "If you have a knife and a screwdriver I can fix it right now. The leak is at the end of the hose."

"Hop down here and let it cool for a moment," said John.

"Just who are you?" Betty asked, naughtily, moving very close to Henry after he hit the ground in front of the truck. She blatantly stared at his muscular arms stretching his tight-fitting T-shirt.

"I heard from a fella in Hays that you all might be hiring, so I stopped by to see about a job." Henry couldn't take his eyes off the pale freckles on her sun-kissed face.

"Do you have a name?" she asked, flashing white teeth.

"Sorry. My name's Henry Dewey."

"Well, Henry Dewey, do you have a place to stay tonight?" she asked.

"Right there in that pickup." He pointed at his beat-up old Chevy.

Betty tilted her head and turned her body in the direction of John. She folded her arms and glared at her brother.

The uncompromising look John gave to Henry made ever so clear that the man meant business.

"Alright, you fix the hose in the truck. Then, you can ride with me on the combine for the rest of the afternoon and I'll see if you can drive this machine." John pulled in a deep breath and stopped to think for a moment. He gave Henry an even more forbidding look. "If, I repeat, if, you can drive the combine, I will hire you, along with giving you a place to stay."

"And food," Betty added.

"Yes, and food," John said agreeably. "But you have to understand that this job isn't going to last very long, we only have about three more weeks of cutting wheat."

"Three weeks is all I need," Henry stated excitedly. The earthy smell of the dry soil mixed with the sweet aroma of wheat dust gave him a sense of belonging. He had always worked in the farm fields, except for the glitch of being in the army. Now, with the sun beating down on his face he knew he was exactly in the place he was supposed to be.

The Harvey farm was resourcefully placed on a hill with wheat fields surrounding it on all sides. A large barn sat about a quarter mile from the main house. With the lack of farm animals, the barn was utilized for the housing of farm machinery and implements. The back area, once used as horse stalls, was remodeled into a lodging area for workers. With a soft bed and a large community bathroom, Henry found the living quarters to be more than adequate.

Although he was tired, and it was late when he finished eating dinner with the other workers, he found it relaxing to sit outside the barn on a stone bench and stare skyward at the bright stars. Expectations had always been low for him, so when he saw Betty strolling across the courtyard in his direction, he thought his heart might beat out of his chest. Arriving about ten feet from him, she stopped walking and looked aloft, with her hands on her hips.

"This sky is so beautiful," she blissfully declared, continuing to gaze into the heavens.

"Not as beautiful as you," Henry thought.

She turned her eyes to focus on him. "Does the cat have your tongue?" she asked coyly.

"No, sorry," he sighed, observing the perfectly cut bangs sitting on her forehead. "I think everything about this farm is beautiful. I'm lucky to have found this place."

"John was bragging at dinner about how fortunate we are to have you here. He was surprised you took to driving the combine so easily." She sat down next to him on the bench.

"That's nice of him. Understanding how machines work has always come naturally to me." He could smell the lotion she put on after showering. Her green eyes sparkled under the starlight.

"You clean up pretty nice." She noticed his hair was slicked back from showering.

"Thank you. So do you. I like your perfume," he stated, smiling.

"What do you like to do besides work?" she impishly inquired. He could feel her left hand moving close to his right hand.

"I like movies," he answered quickly.

"How about cards and other games?" He felt her hand slip into his.

"I like to play cards." He enjoyed the idea of her being aggressive. He gently squeezed her hand.

"How about riding bicycles?"

"I suppose I do, but I haven't ridden one in a long time."

"Can you roller skate?"

"I never have. But something tells me you can."

"I skated professionally at the follies in Denver."

"Then you would skate circles around me." The fact that he was only months from returning from the horrors of war made her asking him questions about everyday life seem encouraging and heartwarming. It was time to look forward and not backward.

"Tomorrow night after dinner, let's go on a bike ride." Betty released his hand and rose to her feet. Without allowing him to confirm the date, she took two steps in the direction of the farmhouse before turning her head to look back. "See you tomorrow."

Sitting in the coolness of the night, knowing it was a farfetched idea, Henry realized that Betty Harvey was the woman of his dreams. He was going to marry her. His heart was beating so hard, with anticipation of all the possibilities that the future might hold with the sister of the farmer, sleep would be difficult, if not impossible.

The next morning, after a night of tossing and turning on his bunk, the anticipation of going to the field to drive the combine was revitalizing. Having a job and a great feeling of hope, not just for the day, but for the future, was something he had wondered if he would ever experience again.

It was a very hot summer day and driving the combine was arduous work. He was able to see Betty on several occasions during the early part of the day when she would pull the wheat truck next to the combine to auger the wheat from the bin into the back of the truck, but they never found a free moment to speak. It only made the expectation of spending time with her in the evening more exciting. Midway through the afternoon Betty was no longer driving the truck. John waited for him in his pickup as he augured the final bin of wheat for the evening.

"Betty must have taken off early today," Henry said to John after parking the combine and joining him in the front seat of the truck for the journey back to the farmhouse.

"She does that sometimes. I can't complain because she is only here because she wants to help me. She has no obligation," John declared.

"Is there anything you can tell me about your sister?" Henry asked.

"Betty is very independent, but beyond that, you will have to figure out who she is on your own."

***

Henry went outside immediately after eating supper to sit on the stone bench in front of the barn. He was outside for only a couple minutes before looking in the direction of the Harvey farmhouse. Betty was pushing two bikes. She was wearing a white blouse with denim pedal pushers. A small backpack was situated on her back.

"Are you ready for a ride?" she asked, pushing the older of the two bikes slightly forward.

"I don't think I have ever been more ready for anything in my life." He took hold of the bike. "This bike looks like it might be an antique."

"John said it is a Van Cleve, which is supposed to be of high quality. I don't have any idea where it came from."

"I've never seen a bike with a handlebar made from wood. I think it's solid oak." He ran his fingers across the smooth wood. He leaned back to get a better vantage point to read a rusty, thin metal plaque situated on the inside of the handlebar.

"What are you looking at?" Betty asked.

"A plate that says the bike came from Pedals Bicycle Shop, Lansing, Michigan, 1897.

"I never noticed that before. It's been sitting in the shed for as long as I can remember, so I'm glad we are going to get some use from it," Betty stated fleetingly. "We need to get going. It's about a four mile ride to the creek."

She straddled her bicycle and took off riding.

"I'm right behind you," Henry yelled, hopping on the bike.

Her muscular calves were visible as she stood up to pedal the bike; he knew it would be a difficult task to keep up. Riding the bicycle was exhilarating. By the time he laid the bike down in the grass next to a creek, his legs were so tired from the unfamiliar exercise he could barely stand.

The creek had deep banks and the evening sun shining off the water created visions of sparkling crosses. Betty placed a thin blanket on the thick green grass next to the embankment of the shallow stream.

"Henry, are you having trouble walking?" She chuckled.

"Maybe a little bit," he said, walking slowly to the edge of the blanket where he lowered his tired body to the coolness of the ground. She sat down next to him.

"It is really beautiful here, Betty," Henry stated as he laid flat on his back.

"I have found this to be a place where I can always come and free my mind." She lay down next to him, allowing her hand to rest on his arm.

Henry sighed. He had never in his life felt so tranquil. All the atrocities of war still situated in the back of his mind disappeared while he stared at the high branches of a giant cottonwood tree glistening in the setting sun. The caress of Betty's hand on his arm, along with the sound of trickling water, took him to an even deeper calm.

"Are you about to fall asleep on me?" Betty asked, leaning over him to place her hand on his chest.

"Never." He turned his head to where he could see her eyes. "I don't want to go to sleep tonight until I know everything there is about you."

"Only if you tell me everything about you."
She sat up and crossed her legs. "You ask first."

He sat up and faced her. "John told me that you are here at the farm to help him for the summer. Where do you live the rest of the time?"

"I grew up here, but now I live in Denver with my mother and little sister, Julie."

"That's pretty far away."

"It's closer than you think. Now, my turn."

"I know your family is in Missouri, I guess what I want to know is," she slapped him on the knee, "do you have a girlfriend or wife back there?"

"No, just my mother, brothers, and sisters," he spoke confidently. "When I returned from Europe it took me a long time to get used to being back with civilized people. Meeting a girl and settling down was all we talked about when we were over there, but when we returned it seemed like it was impossible to meet anyone."

"I lost my fiancé in the war," Betty's voice quivered.

"I'm sorry."

"He was a pilot and was shot down in Italy after being there for only two weeks."

Henry knew that a beauty like her would have many suitors. He moved closer and placed his arm around her. She laid her head on his shoulder, where she rested for a short time, before looking into his eyes. She leaned in and kissed him gently on the lips.

They talked late into the night, telling each other all their deepest and darkest secrets. It was the beginning of what Henry foresaw when he first met Betty. The next three weeks flew by with the two of them spending every vacant moment together. The only issue with time was that there was not enough of it. The night before his last day of driving the combine, Henry proposed to Betty, and she accepted. They married in a little church on the central plains of Kansas before moving to a small farm about forty miles east of Denver, Colorado.

# NINE

Strasburg, Colorado
October 1953

The countryside of eastern Colorado was dry and bare but held a transfixing beauty for those who looked hard enough. Using the GI Bill, and with help from the Harvey family, Betty and Henry were able to purchase a two-hundred-acre farm with a house and small barn on the premises. The house was small, with only two bedrooms, three if you counted the pantry, but it wasn't very old. It was situated on a hill overlooking a grove of cottonwoods with a small creek running across the entirety of their property.

It took seven years for Henry and Betty to have four children, three boys and finally a little girl. It was true love, and they were perfect partners in the life they created. The farm they lived on was constantly in motion. They planted some wheat and raised some cows and chickens, but the children were the real focus of their lives.

"Be very careful with the little chicks," Henry said to Hank Junior, funneling a group of baby chicks from a shallow cardboard box into a pen. He ruffled the red hair on the head of his oldest child.

60

"How long before they have eggs?" Junior was only six years old but already very knowledgeable in farming techniques.

"It will be about three months." He glanced at the freckles on the boy's nose. "Just like his mom," he thought.

"Junior, you need to get out here, right now. It's time for you to go to school." Betty stuck her head into the small chicken coop. She loved how patient and gentle Henry was with the children.

"Look at these little chicks." Junior gently held a chick up in his hand.

"I've seen many chicks before. Put it down, you need to get going to school." Betty smiled at Henry while Junior rushed out the door past her. It was crucial for her to be firm with the children because they all had Henry wrapped around their fingers.

"I spoke with Bill Crider this morning and he said he can get us a television set for under $100.00," Henry stated, looking away conspicuously to fiddle with one of the chicks.

"Why would we want to get a television?" She tapped the side of the chicken coop door with her fingers, waiting for him to answer. "Don't act like you are doing anything with those chicks. I don't understand why we would need a television right now."

"Everyone we know has a television." Henry turned toward her, unable to make a logical reason why they should have a television.

"We are having a hard time keeping up with the bills as it is." She stepped out of the narrow door.

"We are just fine." He followed her out.

"Look over there." Betty pointed to the west where the dark silhouettes of a flock of geese were flying in the bright blue sky. She grabbed hold of his muscular arm and squeezed. "Isn't it beautiful?"

Henry had a flash of despair enter his mind for only a moment from the memory of his time in the army, but when he felt the softness of Betty squeezing his arm, it all disappeared. He stared at the geese flying to the west with the purple out line of Pikes Peak on the horizon.

"The first time we met I knew I was going to marry you," Henry sighed. "Did I ever tell you that I knew from the second I saw you that you were the only one for me?" He stared at her deep green eyes and pink lips. Her beauty was natural, without any make-up.

"I believe you have, several times," she said, leaning her head back.

"You are everything to me, Betty. I never could have imagined, even when we first met, how wonderful life could be."

"Ok, Mr. Dewey, our lives can be even better if I ask Julie to come out this weekend and babysit while you take me to the VFW Hall in Bennett to roller skate."

"Saturday is your birthday, so of course I'll take you skating."

"It will be a celebration."

"I celebrate you all year round." He lifted her up and swung her around. "Believe me, I know how lucky I am."

"So, it's a date."

"You want to go roller skating because you know you are better than everyone in town." He let her slip out of his arms.

"That might be part of the reason," Betty stated agreeably. "I was also thinking I should call Pearl and see if she can meet us at the rink. She has a new man in her life, and it might be a good way to meet him."

"The last time we went out with Pearl you two told stories for more than an hour about working together at Remington Arms during the war. Now I'm not complaining, but I didn't speak over two or three sentences the whole night." Henry smiled at her. "If she does come with a new beau to the roller rink, you have to promise me you will allow him at least one chance to speak during the evening."

"Of course we will," Betty said friskily. "Pearl has been my best friend for many years, and it will be great to see her for my birthday."

"Ok, it is a date. But now I need to get back to work."

Betty pointed to a car slowly moving down their long driveway. "I think it's the Raleigh salesman," she moaned. "I hope he doesn't try and talk our legs off."

"If it is, make sure you don't buy anything we don't need. We ended up with all sorts of junk from him last time," Henry proclaimed.

The 1951 Chevrolet Deluxe sedan pulled right next to Henry and Betty. The man inside held a big smile as he rolled down his window.

"Oh boy," Henry uttered under his breath.

"Can I offer you good folks a large serving of health, happiness and joy?" he queried before exiting his automobile.

The salesman was short and pudgy, with thin, gray hair on top of his round head, combed over from the sides, plastered with so much gel that it flapped up and down from the slight breeze.

"How are you sir?" Betty guardedly asked.

"I was good yesterday, I'm better today, and I'm sure I will be the best I can be tomorrow," he stated. "But what a glorious day it is today."

"We still have one tin of salve left from the last time you were here," Betty quickly specified while glancing at Henry.

Henry sighed.

"I was just telling your neighbors up the road that the Raleigh products continue to improve faster than I can keep track. The new salve has been enhanced from the last time we spoke. That salve was good yesterday, but the ointments I have today are the best in the world."

"I am sure they are. We just don't need any more salve," Betty replied with conviction. She could hear the chickens clucking from the pen behind her.

"Oh, but I have something that will knock your socks right off your feet." He stared at Betty waiting for a response.

"Just what might that be sir?" she hesitantly asked.

"Coconut cream pie mix."

"Sir, I make all my pies from scratch."

"Ok, fair enough. I don't remember if I ever mentioned to you when we spoke before, that I am a true history enthusiast." He glanced over his shoulder at Betty as he opened the back door of his sedan. He pulled out a box full of memorabilia and sat it on the hood of his car.

Henry brought his fingers up and pinched the bridge of his nose. When Betty saw her husband, obviously annoyed, she knew that it would be a short matter of time before the Raliegh man was to be sent on his way, probably in a very abrupt manner.

"I have trinkets, tokens and coins from the 1893 Chicago World's Fair, as well as from other important times in our great country's history." The salesman looked eagerly at Betty. "I have several items of historical importance. I have handbills, posters, and various ticket stubs."

"I really don't think...."

"Look at this," he interrupted Betty, holding up a belt buckle engraved with the words Sam Marciello, middle weight boxing champion Michigan State Fair 1869. "This is solid silver. But more important is that it was found with items belonging to Leon Czolgosz."

He looked with great anticipation, directly at Henry.

"Who the hell is Leon Czolgosz?" Henry loudly asked, trying his best to pronounce the name correctly.

"He's the guy that shot President Mckinley," yelled the salesman loudly, flopping his arms to his side.

"I didn't know President Mckinley was ever shot."

"Of course he was shot. He was assassinated," the Raliegh salesman screeched with a loud, preachy manner that implied Henry must be uneducated for not knowing such a bygone fact. "That's the reason Theodore Roosevelt became president."

"Why in the world would I want that belt buckle?"

"For God's sake man, it's a part of history," he loudly yelled. He took a step back with his mouth open, glaring at Henry.

"You're about to become a part of history." Henry grabbed the box off the hood of the car and tossed it into the back seat. "Now you have one minute to get off my land."

The salesman scowled at Henry as he retreated to his car. He spun the tires as he drove off.

Betty started laughing.

"Well, now I'll get back to work," Henry said with a smile.

# TEN

The Veterans of Foreign Wars Quonset style building was already packed by the time Betty and Henry entered the large open room. Betty carried her high top, leather roller skates. The inside of the VFW Hall was huge with hardwood floors and arched lacquered, wooden beams spaced across the length of the structure. People were already roller skating with many spectators standing next to the wall.

They acknowledged several of the local townspeople while making their way to the back concession area, hoping to find a table. All the spaces were occupied but far in the back corner Pearl was standing by a table, waving. Sitting next to her was a small man wearing wire-rimmed glasses.

"Pearl, you beat us here." Betty maneuvered around the tables trying not to bang on people with her skates. She gave her friend a hug.

"We've been here for an hour. Lucky we did because we got the last table." Pearl wore bright red lipstick that made the large freckles on her high cheek bones stand out even more than usual. She turned to Henry and put her arms out. "Give me a hug, you big, beautiful hunk of a man."

Henry chuckled and gave her a hug. "Glad to see you, Pearl."

"This is Bernard Whitley," Pearl spoke with her arm remaining around Henry's waist.

"Nice to meet you all. I've heard a lot about you," replied Bernard affably. He was a slight man with a shadow of a beard. The glasses he wore were much thicker than they appeared from a distance.

"Nice to meet you, Bernard." Betty held out her hand and shook his tiny hand. She placed her roller skates under the table next to Pearl's skates.

Henry pulled himself from the grip of Pearl. He sat directly across from the new beau because he knew that Betty and Pearl would completely tune out the two men if they were allowed to sit next to each other. This way they would have to talk across the table and wouldn't be able to exclude the men. He was wrong. The two women conversed as if nobody else was in the room.

Henry and Bernard went to the concession stand and bought drinks. The ladies were still talking when they returned. They made feeble efforts to bring the men into the conversation for the next thirty minutes. Finally, they stopped.

"Shall we go roller skate?" Betty turned her focus away from Pearl and looked at Henry. She began to lace up her roller skates.

"I'm ready," said Pearl, reaching down to grab her roller skates from under the table.

"If you don't mind, Betty, I think I will just watch you two skate," Henry stated, clenching his teeth, waiting for her to deny him.

"I'm feeling the same way," expressed Bernard.

Betty glanced at Pearl as her friend finished putting on her skates. Pearl shrugged.

"You two enjoy yourself," Betty said, leaning over to give Henry a kiss on his cheek.

The two women maneuvered around the tables and out onto the roller rink.

"Henry, Pearl told me you were with the 99th Infantry in the war." Bernard placed both of his hands on the table.

"Yes." Henry's eyes inadvertently lowered.

"Sorry if I am overreaching here. I know most veterans don't like speaking about their service," stated Bernard. "I saw the horror myself."

"I'm sorry you had to experience it." Henry looked him directly in the eyes. "Who were you with?"

"I worked in intelligence with the Office of Strategic Services."

"I didn't figure you to be a grunt." Henry smiled at him.

"I'm trained as a psychiatrist." Bernard smiled back.

"I'm sure there is a lot of need for that now."

"I was hoping I would get a chance to speak with you tonight. Pearl told me how you and Betty have adapted to family life. I find it refreshing how you acclimated back to civilian life," Bernard sighed. "Henry, you need to cherish every single moment you have with your family. Focus on them, not on the past."

Henry never spoke of the atrocities he witnessed during the war, not with Betty, nor with anyone else. He only shared that he was in the 99th Infantry stationed in Belgium. The black notebook he kept during the war, along with some pictures, his medals and dog tags were neatly put away in a drawer in their bedroom. Although the carnage of war was something he never figured to be talking about on his date night with Betty, the caring psychiatrist gave him a tremendous sense of relief.

"I know I'm fortunate," proclaimed Henry.

"If you ever need someone to talk to, maybe over a beer or cup of coffee, please feel free to give me a call."

"I appreciate that." He noticed Bernard looking past his shoulder.

"Pearl is yelling at us." Bernard stood up and pointed in the direction of the roller rink.

"Henry, hurry, we need your help," Pearl yelled from the edge of the tables. "There is some big palooka out here harassing Betty."

"Oh, my gosh."

Henry rushed through the tables to the rink. An extremely large man with a blackened eye and a fresh scar a couple inches long on his bald head, rocked back and forth on his roller skates. He was arguing with Betty. Everybody had stopped skating and were gathered around.

"It's ok. We are just having a little disagreement," Betty disclosed calmly to Henry when he arrived at her side.

"Yeah, this stumblebum has been bothering us ever since we started skating," declared Pearl, taking hold of Bernard's hand.

"I was just telling the pretty ladies that they are good skaters, but not as good as me," avowed the man, mockingly. A mischievous grin was on his arrogant face. He was the type who wore the scar on his head with pride. "I only want to race."

"Listen, the ladies are here to have some fun skating without being troubled by you," stated Henry sternly. He wasn't threatened at all by the man as he looked at the bloke's flattened nose. "Now you get on your way and let everyone get back to skating."

"I'm not going anywhere."

Henry momentarily stared at him, contemplating the best way to peacefully calm the situation without ruining their night out. He realized that if he stayed calm, everyone around him would do the same.

"I want to race. After I beat the lady with the fancy skates, then I'll leave."

Henry turned to Betty and whispered in her ear, "Can you beat him?"

"In a heartbeat," she whispered back, with a big smile on her face, enjoying the entire situation. Her smile was contagious and soon most of the people gathered around were also smiling.

"Ok, if it's alright with everyone, let's have a race." Henry held his hands out palms up.

"Five times around the oval," suggested Betty, glancing at the brute.

"Five times is perfect for me."

Four cones were placed at each end of the rink. Betty didn't argue with the man when he insisted on being on the inside to begin the race. It was obvious from the start that he was overmatched. She easily beat him to the first cone and skated around the oval far ahead on the beginning lap.

Henry kept an eye on the bully with Bernard and Pearl waiting by his side. After three laps the spectators became very loud and soon began heckling the large gent as Betty was ready to catch him. On the fourth lap around the oval, she caught him and began to go around. He stopped and swung his arm out forcefully, trying to clothesline her. She went to one knee, sliding easily under his arm and around him.

Henry rushed out onto the rink and pulled the man by the back of his shirt. The big fellas' legs flew high into the air, and he landed hard on his backside. He was up in a hurry. Bernard stepped in between the two men.

"Let's settle this amicably." Bernard held the back of his hand on the bully's chest with one finger pointing at his chin. "Sir, you were beaten solidly and very fair...."

Whap. The man punched the small psychiatrist right on the nose. Henry stepped in and pummeled the obviously inebriated man until several local men stopped the fight. They tossed the stranger to the street, still wearing his roller skates.

"Are you ok?" Betty could see a small bruise under Henry's eye. She had never seen her mild-mannered husband so irate. Deep down she was delighted that this calm man would fight for her.

"Betty, it's still your birthday," said Pearl, putting her arm around Bernard, who was holding a handkerchief to his nose. "Let's go to the café and have some cake."

"How about we go to the bar instead?" Bernard recommended with a muffled voice, looking at the blood on his hands.

"Betty has never had a drink of alcohol in her entire life," interjected Pearl, "I don't think she wants to start now."

"I'm good with going to the bar, I can drink a coke. I think these guys deserve a drink," Betty stated.

"Happy Birthday." Henry leaned in and gave her a kiss.

Henry was proud of Betty's coolness and grit when she found herself confronted by the tormentor. She was always in control of any situation, and she did so with a big smile on her face. For the rest of the night, he couldn't stop staring at her, with her beautiful red hair pulled back in a ponytail, laughing and hugging with

her friend. He was lucky to have a wife with
such a great understanding of the little joys in
life.

# ELEVEN

Father's Day was a day Henry cherished. It was a time where he could spend the entire day with his family. Betty was terrific at taking care of the early morning chores of feeding and tending to the animals that were necessary on the farm, allowing him to sleep late.

The children were not so forgiving to their father. They wanted him up and available to play. By the time Betty returned from feeding the chickens, Henry was outside on the lawn playing baseball with Junior, John, and Daniel, while Kaye lay in a wooden bassinet on the porch.

Betty stopped at the outside of the fence surrounding the large grass lawn in front of the house to watch her family play. Henry helped Daniel hold a baseball bat, which was too large for the boy, who was a few months away from being three years old, while Junior tossed the ball over a worn-out T-shirt being used as home plate. John waited patiently at another old T-shirt being used as first base, watching his older brother concentrate to throw the hard baseball across home base without hitting his father and little brother. Henry's easy-going disposition helped him maneuver around the different and unique personalities of each of his children.

Betty entered the gate, making sure to walk around the baseball game in progress to get to the bassinet on the porch. She held Kaye while watching the boys play, noticing white clouds in the sky over the mountains.

"Henry, it looks like a storm might be brewing up in the west," she said anxiously.

Henry glanced past the cottonwood on the outside of the fence in the direction of the thunderheads. "Something is coming in. We are about done playing anyway."

"I'm hungry!" yelled John.

"Didn't you eat breakfast?" Betty asked.

"Yes, we all ate toast and cereal before we came out," Henry quantified with a sharp look towards John.

"I'll make some sandwiches for lunch," replied Betty, staring up towards the blue sky with the hot sun pouring down on her face. She could see the line of clouds in the west rolling toward the farm. "With it being so hot this morning, I think we can expect this storm to be pretty bad."

"I'll keep an eye on it," said Henry.

"I have an angel food cake with chocolate fudge frosting that we can eat after lunch," Betty stated with a large smile on her face.

"Sounds delicious." Henry helped Daniel swing the bat while looking at Junior. "Go ahead and toss us a couple more."

"Can we play hide and seek?" Junior asked, before a low rumble of thunder came from the west.

"No, I want to play Chutes and Ladders."

"Whatever we play, we'll have to play it inside. We are about to have a bad storm." Henry picked up Daniel and moved toward the front door.

Henry had the boys go to the living room while he remained at the front porch, watching the rapidly developing storm. The sky was a deep blue with flashes of lightning continuously visible. Betty joined him outside.

"It seems to be an awfully strong storm," stated Betty anxiously.

"It really brewed up fast. Where is Kaye?"

"I put her in the crib."

"Maybe it would be best to keep her in the bassinet just in case we need to hurry down to the cellar," stated Henry.

"Oh, I hope it doesn't get bad enough for us to have to go into that dreadful place," said Betty just as a huge gust of wind blew the screen door shut.

"I'm going to make sure the door to the barn is latched tight." Henry took off in a full sprint out the gate to the yard.

"Hurry!" Betty yelled before stepping inside the house.

The pitter-patter of raindrops striking the front window soon turned into a loud hammering sound as small bits of hail struck the side of the house. Betty placed Kaye in the bassinet and moved the boys nearer to the door, going down to the cellar. Henry burst through the front door.

"Go to the cellar," he shouted. "There's a tornado just to the south."

Betty flipped on the light and carried Kaye down the narrow concrete steps into the dark cellar, followed closely by the three boys. Henry momentarily stayed in the living room before slamming the door shut and rushing down next to his family.

The basement was small with concrete block walls, covered by wood shelves on three sides. The light gave out a low amount of illumination making the dreary room feel even smaller.

"Oh Lord, please don't let the tornado hit a farm." Betty glanced at Henry.

"There ain't a thing we can do about it," replied Henry quietly. "If the tornado hits our place, we will put it all back together."

"Will it suck us out of here?" asked Junior.

"No, it won't suck us up," said Henry confidently, but we will definitely know if it does hit our house."

"We will have to wait here as a family for a little longer. The longer we wait without something happening, the better," said Betty.

"The storm was moving really fast." Henry took a couple steps up the cellar steps. "I'll go up and check."

The kids and Betty could hear Henry trouncing around on the living room floor above them, with dust filling the air with each of his steps. He quickly moved to the cellar door and yelled down, "The storm has passed, you can come up."

It was cold outside when they moved out the front door to survey the damage. Hail was mixed with green leaves from the cottonwood tree covering the front lawn. No windows were broken, but big chunks of siding lay in the dirt at the bottom of the foundation.

"I think we dodged a bullet here," said Henry elatedly.

"Look at this," said Junior, holding up a hail stone as big as the baseball they were playing with earlier.

Both Henry and Betty were familiar with tornadic storms, and they knew from the size of the hail stone that they were lucky the worst of the storm passed them by.

***

Betty came out of the kids' bedroom and sat down next to Henry on the couch. He opened his arms and allowed her to lay with her head on his chest.

"They are all asleep," she said, moving her eyes to look up while continuing with her head on his chest.

"I was surprised the storm didn't knock out the electricity." He squeezed her shoulder.

"That was quite a Father's Day, wasn't it?" she said, continuing to look up.

"I like it when you move your eyes that way."

"What way?"

"You know. Up without moving your head." Henry chuckled. "You did it the first time we met and probably a hundred times since."

"Mr. Dewey likes it when I do this?" She twisted her head away and looked at him seductively.

"We have four kids, don't we?"

She hesitated.

"We do have four kids," he repeated.

"I guess I should tell you. I'm not one hundred percent positive, but I think we are about to have number five."

Henry sat up. "I guess that answers your question, I very much like it when you look at me that way."

"Are you happy?" she asked.

"I don't think it would be possible for me to be happier." He spoke with a more serious tone. "But Betty, with another mouth to feed, I think I need to take a job."

"We can make ends meet. The wheat harvest will be starting in about three weeks." Betty sat straight up.

"Several of the other farmers have been working as roughnecks on the oil rigs," he sighed. "I know I can get a job immediately. I figure if I work three weeks before harvest begins, I can make enough money to keep our heads above water."

"Oh, Henry, I don't know."

"You can take care of feeding the animals. I would be accomplishing nothing for the next few weeks by sitting around here. I might as well be making some extra money."

"I guess you're right," Betty stated hesitantly.

***

Henry was up by five in the morning and finished feeding the farm animals by six. The oil rig he took the job on was about forty-five minutes to the north of the farm. He rushed inside the house and grabbed his lunch box.

"Are you excited about going to work?" Betty asked.

"Not really. But we will like the extra money." He noticed Betty's face was flushed a bright pink.

"What time will you be back?"

"I suppose around six or so." He opened the door to the kid's bedroom and crept in to give each of them a kiss on their cheeks.

"If you're supposed to be on the job by seven, you better get going," Betty said sternly.

He leaned in and gave her a kiss on the mouth. "You look beautiful today."

"Get going," she said with a chuckle. "I love you."

"Love you, too."

He spun the tires as he exited the dirt driveway to the farm. By the time he reached the county road he was going as fast as the automobile could go. He had the gas pedal to the floorboard. The dirt road he was traveling on was straight but narrow. His mind was on everything but driving. By the time he noticed a large pothole in the middle of the road it was too late to slow down. He jerked the steering wheel and the wheels on the right side of the car were caught in the soft side of the bar ditch. The car flipped and the driver's side door opened, and he fell out. He looked up as the car came tumbling down on top of him.

# TWELVE

A blinding white light triggered Henry to slam his eyes shut. When he opened them, he was sitting on a bench in front of a crystal-clear river running through a park of bright green lawns and trees. The sky was perfect Cerulean blue. An older lady sat close by him with her arms crossed.

"No, this can't be. I can't be here," Henry yelled frantically.

"Sit back and take a deep breath," commanded the old lady with a gravelly voice. "Everything is just fine."

"I'm dead."

"Yep, your dead," she said gruffly.

"No. How could I die and leave my little children and wife in such terrible circumstances? I'm a good person."

"You were driving too fast." She cleared her throat. "Just lean back and breath. Everything will be alright."

"Send me back! Send me back now!" he screamed.

"We can't send you back. It's over," the lady spoke firmly with an unyielding tone.

"I have four small children and a pregnant wife. For me," he groaned, "to die at this time is not fair."

"Stop whining. Fairness has never been guaranteed to anyone. Just relax."

"What? If I remember right, you are supposed to be comforting me, and bringing me to a place of blessedness?"

"That's what I am attempting to do. Now, if you will be quiet and listen to what I am saying, I can help bring you tranquility," her raspy voice was infuriating.

"You shut up. Send me back now."

"Really," her voice sounded like she had just swallowed a teaspoon of silica sand.

"Yeah, really."

"Why don't you give me a little slack here. You know it's not easy telling people they are dead," she pleaded.

"It's ok, Henry," the illuminated image of a lady standing in the distance spoke with a comforting tone.

"Mom," said Henry. "It's not right that I have to leave my family."

"We'll be able to talk in just a while." Her image disappeared.

"I need the card in your shirt pocket," declared the lady with a rough voice. "I'll get you to the floor you should be on, something tells me they are going to readjust your numerical standing. If they don't, they should."

The overwhelming sense of loss and remorse continued as Henry entered a room with walls of bright pastel colors. He couldn't stop thinking about Betty and his little children having to endure the thought of him never returning. He was surprised he could recall so much of the process he was now experiencing. Everything about the room was the same as he remembered, including the enrapturing lady sitting behind the glass desk.

"Why would you do this, to not only me, but to my family, my children? Why would you take it all away from me after I lived every part of my life in a virtuous way?"

"The question of why dreadful occurrences happen to good people has been asked forever. Promises are very few, here and on earth. You were never guaranteed that by being a good person that something you deem to be bad would never happen. Your family on earth is just fine."

"It's not fair."

"You found true love with a beautiful family. So, what is not fair? You are not seeing the larger picture of who you are."

"To take it all away. They were my whole world. Why would this happen?"

"Do you believe that your love for Betty should have been for eternity?"

He hesitated before answering, "Maybe, I don't know."

"If you do, the only way to satisfy your belief in fairness would be for both of you to live together in harmony forever."

"I am more worried about my family than I am about myself. It's not right to leave them to survive without me."

"As I said before, they are fine. The shortness of life experiences is a reason your angels constantly remind you to live every moment of your life as if it is your last."

"It is so hard leaving them." He took a deep breath and released; the pain was nearly all gone. "I am sorry for how I acted. Please tell the greeter that I apologize, and I know I was out of line."

"She has no hard feelings; she can handle a little rudeness. Your passion for life is wonderful. The spirit within you to live is what makes you so special. A zest for life is looked upon very highly here."

He sighed.

"Do you have any questions? You can ask about anything. Questions are good. But remember they will be answered specifically in the way you ask them."

"Why do I exist? What is the purpose?"

"I don't understand how you could ask that question after finding the love you found. Your life was well lived, and you found your purpose in family and love. You have your own purpose, different from others. Everyone has the freedom to construct their own meaning."

"I went through a war and saw the very worst of what humans are capable of doing to one another."

"Evil does exist."

"Why does it have to exist?"

"It is not of our making. Humans must make the choice between good and evil. Believe me, there are people on earth who have experienced far worse than you have."

"Don't you have the power to make everything good?" he asked. "I witnessed terrible suffering during the war."

"No. Life grows or shrinks depending on the choices made, even when facing the most unbearable of situations. Everyone has the freedom to make their own choices and bear the consequences or reap the rewards. Life on earth would become stagnant if everything was given to humanity. The world owes you nothing, but the possibility for everything exists."

"I witnessed the aftermath of so many people dying from human cruelty without any chance to make a choice as to their fate. Why would this happen?"

"Humans made the choice to perpetrate the atrocities."

"Are humans evil?"

"Of course they are not. Look at yourself, your life reflects much of humanity's goodness. You are moral, loving, and compassionate. You yourself fought to stop the wickedness of others. But I will say that it pains us terribly up here when we witness carnage and mayhem on earth."

"Can I meet with my angels?"

"Of course you can. I must tell you that you have an exceptional group of angels."

"Even when I was on earth, I sensed their presence."

"They are there to help you. Now is the time to make known to them your greatest desires. What name do you want when you go back?"

"I want to be named Aaron."

"Good choice. Go speak with your angels."

The doors to the side of the room opened. He walked through the door into a beautiful bright light.

# THIRTEEN

Denver, Colorado
March 1989

Aaron Jackson considered himself to be an average man, a normal person, but one with great aspirations, although these ambitions were avoiding him like the plague. He wasn't handsome, but he wasn't homely, he wasn't tall, but he wasn't short, and he certainly wasn't rich, but he wasn't homeless either. His easygoing demeanor allowed him to use the commonality he shared with his fellow citizens to understand the needs and wants of the populace, something valuable in marketing and advertising.

As an adjunct professor, on a one-semester contract at Ellis Community College, he had the liberty to make decisions for his future without being weighed down with any set responsibilities. As much as he cherished his station of freedom in life, he was trying his hardest to change his status; by finding a secure job, and he planned to marry Sarah, his girlfriend of over two years.

Warm days and May flowers were blooming, creating a sense of change. Because he had not received a new contract from the college for the fall semester, he figured that the session he was teaching would be his final at the institution.

He paced back and forth in front of the class of twenty students. His classroom was situated in the windowless interior of the school, a blessing on this beautiful spring day that the students couldn't look outside and fantasize about being somewhere else besides Marketing 101.

"Nostalgia," Aaron shouted, leaning on the edge of the desk in front of the class. "Can someone tell me how this might be important to an advertising firm?"

He surveyed the classroom. All the students were paying attention. He noticed an older lady sitting at the back of the room who was not one of his students. Nobody raised their hands.

"Come on, we are coming to the end of this class. Someone should have an idea of why nostalgia is important in advertising." A student in the second row raised her hand. It was Mary, one of his favorite pupils who always was willing to listen and participate. "Yes, girl with the pink stripe in her hair."

"Mr. Jackson, you know my name's Mary," she said with a grin. "The reason is because people can have memories where they yearn for their past selves. Positive emotions from seeing a product will make them want to buy it."

"Very well done Mary." He smiled back at her. "There is a reason why you must take classes in history, psychology, and other curriculums to get a degree in marketing. Understanding history and the emotions associated with the times can be very powerful in promoting."

"Some things in the past have bad memories, too," stated a student.

"Of course they do, Anthony. Sometimes terrible circumstances from the past can be a compelling way to sell. Can you tell me how a bad situation would benefit an advertiser?"

"Maybe having a car crash if you are emphasizing the safety of the car you are selling," stated Anthony.

"I don't think you would want to show the car crashing if you are trying to get people to buy it."

"How about showing a tornado or fire for an insurance company," said a man from the back of the room. "Being reliable and helping the people during a disaster is a reason people would want to buy the insurance. It would also make a consumer think about how vulnerable they would be during a disaster if they didn't have insurance."

"Absolutely. The trick is to create an ad that makes people want to buy the product because they feel safe, accepted by others, or even secure. Advertising has changed a lot over the past ten years. Telling a story with a catch phrase now seems to be the standard used in the industry. The problem is that the meaning of the story needs to be conveyed to the public in about thirty seconds," Aaron spoke confidently. "Most good ads are developed through a team approach, so what I want to do now is break into groups of four or five. The product we are promoting is tires. I want a thirty-second story from each group that would be good for a television advertisement. There is about an hour and a half left in class, so you have thirty minutes to construct your advertisement. Then we will take the final hour of class for presentations."

Aaron sat down on his office chair behind his desk as the clattering sound of chairs filled the room. He kept an eye on the mysterious lady at the back of the classroom. She sat with her head down, patiently writing in a notepad. While he still had eyes on her, she stood up and walked to the front of the room. She placed her right hand on the edge of his desk.

"Mr. Jackson," she said affably, "my name is Charlotte Machiado. I represent Avery Marketing Company and would like to speak with you about an opening we have coming available."

"I'm surprised you would do this during my class," Aaron declared apprehensively. He was familiar with the large company. It recently received a lot of press in the tabloids concerning the health of the flamboyant owner of the company. She was the American daughter of Nigerian-born parents who was known for outlandish behavior in running the very successful company. Beyond that, he knew very little about the internal operations of the business.

"Seeing in person your approach to teaching was my final evaluation," she stated with certainty. "The opportunity for this job I offer to you is for only a select few."

"Are you offering me a job without an interview?" Aaron noticed the lady was older than she appeared at first. She possessed gracefulness, a refinement that made her compelling and believable.

"Yes, I am offering you employment. There will be an interview to determine at what level in the company you fit."

"This is very unorthodox," his voice lowered. He glanced at the students who were busy working in groups. He timidly looked back at her and asked, "Are you sure you have the right guy?"

"Yes, I'm sure," she chuckled. "We have already vetted you. You have been evaluated and found to be exactly who we would like to offer employment."

"This couldn't come at a better time for me. This class is coming to an end, and I haven't received a contract for next year," he declared. "Also, I am planning on getting married in the near future."

"I know everything there is to know about you," she boldly specified. She handed him a card. "The time and location for the interview are on the card. We look forward to seeing you there."

His eyes followed her as she left the room. The business card had edges outlined with gold ink, and felt as though it was made from leather rather than paper.

# FOURTEEN

Aaron looked at the heavy makeup around the pretty saleswoman's eyes before turning his gaze back to the glass counter where three diamond rings sat on a black cloth.

"I am torn between the white gold solitaire setting and the cathedral ring setting. There is really a large difference in price," he indicated with a questioning tone to his voice as he stared at the rings.

"The difference in a ring depends on the girl you are giving it to. Is she plain and ordinary, or is she the ornate and elegant type?"

He shot her a glance. Her smile was stamped on her face. He didn't appreciate the salesmanship, but she did hit a nerve. He would feel guilty for getting Sarah a cheap ring.

"I'll take the cathedral ring setting."

"Good choice," the saleswoman said, snatching the ring before quickly placing the other rings under the counter. "I'll package this up and be right back."

"Is this ring guaranteed?" he yelled at her.

"Guaranteed from what?" she asked, turning to look back at him with a puzzled look.

"I don't know, maybe from turning green on my fiancée's finger."

"I will guarantee it won't turn green on her finger." She shook her head before proceeding to the back.

***

He held the box with the ring firmly in his hand as he ran two blocks down the street to the café where a meeting was previously planned with his best friend, Arnold Swisher. Arnold was sitting in a booth near the entrance patiently waiting his arrival.

"How's going?" He couldn't wait to tell him about his purchase.

"What are you so excited about?" asked Arnold. The jowls on his chubby face jiggled as he watched Aaron slip into the seat across from him.

"I did it."

"Did what?"

"I bought Sarah a ring." He pulled the ring out of the box and held it inches from Arnold's face. "I am going to ask her to marry me tomorrow."

"Oh man. You are taking a big chance. You should ask her in private," Arnold groaned.

"I want the proposal to be special, something we will be able to remember forever."

"Take her up in the mountains and propose looking at the lights of the city."

"I'm doing it tomorrow at her sister's birthday party," Aaron insisted. "Her entire family can be a part of this moment. You know her dad likes me a lot."

"You're not asking her dad to marry you," Arnold specified sarcastically.

"I'm going to be thirty years old in a few months. You've been married for over ten years." He stared at the receding hairline on his friend who most people would consider to be quite homely. "You took a chance in asking Elizebeth to marry you, and that worked out pretty well."

"I want to be honest. You and Sarah are on different levels professionally, socially, and every other way I can think. She has a high paying job at the bank, and her parents are rich." Arnold lowered his voice and glanced at the other people sitting in the next booth over. "I don't think you are ready to get married. You don't have any money saved and you are a part-time teacher at a community college. For God's sake, you live in a one-bedroom apartment in a building that looks like it will blow over in a heavy windstorm."

"I wanted to tell you; I have a job set up with Avery Advertising Company."

"That's great! What position?" He was surprised, and a little bit skeptical, but guardedly happy for his friend.

"I definitely have the job," Aaron declared awkwardly. "I'm meeting with them next Friday and will find out exactly where I fit in."

"I'm proud of you, man," Arnold's voice was anything but reassuring. "Why don't you wait until the job is confirmed before asking Sarah to marry you?"

"I need to stop procrastinating and do it now. Sarah knows I have been spinning my wheels." Aaron leaned closer. "She told me that I have more potential than anyone she has ever met, and now with this job I can prove it to her."

"What the hell are you thinking?" Arnold spoke louder than he intended. "If you told me she said you were the light of her life, and she couldn't live without you, I would say she is the woman for you. But she told you that you have potential. Come on."

"Maybe you needed to hear the tone of her voice when she said it."

"She's out of your league," Arnold strongly proclaimed. "You won't be happy with her, and you will never have a moment's peace in your life, if, for some great miracle, she does accept your proposal."

"You don't want me to get married because then I won't be around to fix your car, or your chain saw, or your lawn mower, or anything else that breaks around your house."

"That is ridiculous. Just order something to eat."

"I have too much to do before the party." Aaron stood up and took a step away from the booth before turning around. "You and Elizebeth are going to be at the party, right?"

"We wouldn't miss it for the world," Arnold sighed.

"I'll see you there."

"Wait!" Arnold spoke with a sense of urgency. "If you feel you need to propose, please make sure you do it sober."

"Of course I will."

# FIFTEEN

Sarah's family home was located on a large lot in the exclusive Cherry Hills area of greater Denver. The food for the party was placed in the indoor dining area with most of the party events being held in the large backyard. A bandstand was situated in the far back corner of the lawn.

Aaron stepped around several partygoers on the well-manicured grass before seeing Sarah standing under a large canopy, dramatically telling a story to a small group of people. She was dressed in a white pantsuit, with her auburn-colored hair pulled back on the left side, leaving one wild strand of hair to fall over her forehead, causing her to constantly push it away from her eyes. Two of the women and one of the men she was talking with were coworkers of hers he recognized from the bank, but the other man was a stranger. The box with the ring in the front pocket of his slacks bulged out as he moved under the shelter.

Sarah greeted him with a smile but continued telling her story. The focus of her storytelling was in the direction of the stranger, who was quite tall and dressed in a Christian Dior herringbone double breasted suit. Aaron recognized that the suit was worth more than he had in his bank account, especially since he just bought Sarah the expensive ring.

"Aaron," Sarah said loftily. "I want you to meet Stanley Blake."

"Nice to meet you." He firmly shook the stranger's hand. "Are you new to town? I don't believe we have ever met."

"Oh no, I've worked with Sarah for about three months at the bank," stated Stanley haughtily without looking him in the eyes. His demeanor toward Aaron was dismissive.

"I'm sure there are a lot of people I haven't met at Sarah's work." Aaron slipped his hand into Sarah's, smiling at her other co-workers, who all seemed apprehensive with his presence.

"Are Arnold and Elizebeth coming to the party?" Sarah asked tepidly, looking past Aaron in the direction of the house. She pulled her hand out of his and put on a pair of sunglasses outlined with silver sparkles.

"Yes, they are. I can't believe they aren't here yet."

"Looks like my parents are preparing to sing happy birthday to Marcella. I guess I should go and see if they need any help with the cake."

Aaron sensed a disconnect from Sarah. Instead of following her to the house to hear everyone sing happy birthday to her sister, he walked across the lawn to the stage where band members were setting up to perform. Sarah was always moody and sometimes irritable with him, but she seemed even more detached than usual. He stared blankly at the blades of green grass, with the sun shining from them, completely lost in his thoughts.

"You look like your dog just died," said a young man with long, straight hair, wearing a blue T-shirt with a picture of a surfer riding a wave.

"What was that?" Aaron turned to the man who was sitting on the edge of the stage.

"I was saying, you look really down."

"No, no, I'm not depressed or anything like that." He took a couple of steps in the young man's direction. The sound of people singing Happy Birthday echoed in the distance.

"Maybe not, man, but your jaw looks like it's hanging on the ground. Life's too short for you to come to a party and beat up on yourself."

"I'm really not beating up on myself," he responded defensively. "I'm just nervous and unsure of the best approach to asking someone to marry me."

"Love is all you need," the young man sang the words, pounding a couple of times on the stage with his fingertips.

"Love is what I am hoping to find," replied Aaron with a big smile.

"I'm more of a money, money, money type guy," he chuckled. "Who's the lucky lady?"

"Sarah, the sister of the birthday girl." He put his hand out to the stranger. "By the way, my name's Aaron. "Are you with the band?"

"Yeah, I'm the drummer." He gave a quick squeeze of Aaron's hand but didn't give his name. "Is the sister the lady in the white pantsuit?"

"Yeah, that's her."

"Aaron," yelled Arnold.

He turned to see Arnold walking cautiously on the thick lawn, with Elizebeth on his arm.

"You missed the birthday song," Arnold stated.

"I'm a little nervous." He gave Elizebeth a quick hug. "How are you doing?"

"Fine," she said, gently rubbing his shoulder. "Arnold told me all about you buying Sarah a ring."

"I'm excited about my decision, but still a little unsure about the best way to go about it." He always considered Arnold to be a lucky man because of the confidence and sensuality of Elizebeth. She was far from being a raging beauty, but her buoyancy and poise made her special.

"What's your plan?" asked Elizebeth.

"I just met the drummer for the band," Aaron motioned to the young man who was still sitting on the edge of the stage. "I'm contemplating having the band pause after a song and announce that I want to ask someone a very important question."

All three of them stared at the drummer. He was gritting his teeth, looking away from them. It was obvious he could hear them talking.

"Do you think you could find a time somewhere during the first set to introduce me to the crowd so I can propose?" Aaron looked directly at the drummer and spoke loudly. "This sounds like the best way for me to get everyone's attention."

"I don't know, man. I don't think that's a good idea." He flipped his long hair back and shook his head. He was obviously distressed as he looked down at his shoes.

"What's the problem?" asked Arnold, surprised the young musician would hesitate to help with the engagement announcement.

"Let me verify something before I spill my guts," quantified the drummer, slipping away from the stage to stand next to Aaron. "You already told me that the sister of the birthday girl you plan to give a ring to is wearing a white pantsuit. I just want to clarify that she is the tall brunette wearing the funky silver sunglasses."

"Yeah, that's her," Aaron guardedly affirmed.

"You seem like a good guy, so I will tell you this to save you from making a terrible mistake. I saw her and a guy in an expensive suit on the back side of the stage when I brought my drums in earlier this morning." He hesitated for a moment before continuing. "Man, I'm sorry to tell you this, but the rich guy had his tongue stuck down her throat. They were there for quite a while, and they weren't talking."

Aaron was at a loss for words. He turned away from Elizebeth and Arnold. He sensed everything he was told by the drummer was the truth.

"It's not the end of the world," declared Arnold sympathetically.

"This is pretty humiliating." The box with the ring rubbing against his leg added to the humbling situation. He turned to Arnold. "You were right. She is out of my league."

"I wish I wasn't," surmised Arnold.

"Why don't we leave. We'll go with you, and you can hash this out with Sarah at a better time," said Elizebeth. "Don't make a bad situation worse by making a scene."

"I feel a little sick. I agree we should leave."

# SIXTEEN

The next day, Sarah confessed that she had been in a relationship with her coworker for more than a month. In her words, "they had drifted apart." Being at the tail end of his teaching contract at the community college, losing his girlfriend, and realizing his living conditions at the dilapidated apartment were despicable, challenged Aaron to question every decision he had made in life.

Arnold and Elizebeth were available for him to cry on their shoulders, but their support could only be taken so far. Being a loser and having your best friend and his wife realize just how big a failure you were, was hard to bear. Eating, drinking, and even sleeping were difficult. He never felt so sad and alone as he did that week leading to his interview with the marketing firm.

Skipping the interview was an option he would have chosen had the meeting been a few days earlier. Time has a way of healing even a broken heart. On the day of the interview, Aaron lay in the middle of his bed on a worn and lumpy mattress, flat on his back glaring at the putrid, smoke-stained, popcorn ceiling. The moldy air sat heavily in his nostrils. When he became motivated enough to sit up, he stared mindlessly at the floral wallpaper peeling away from the drywall. He went through the motions of dressing in black slacks, a white shirt with a tan sports jacket, and no tie.

The gathering for potential employees was held in an enclosed room at the back of an upscale restaurant near downtown Denver. By the time Aaron arrived, twelve people were already sitting around a table with drinks and desserts in front of them. He was right on time, but there was a terrible feeling that he was late. A fleeting thought entered his mind that he wasn't worthy of being with these people since all of them took it upon themselves to be early for the interview. He sat down next to a man in a very nice suit who politely nodded. Charlotte, the lady who came to his classroom to offer him the job, was nowhere to be seen.

"Alright, let us get started," said a middle-aged lady, standing at the opposite side of the round table. She had chocolate brown hair and was finely dressed in stylish clothes. She held up her left hand to display perfectly manicured pink fingernails, and a wedding ring with a large diamond setting. Speaking in a calm and confident voice she announced, "My name is Jacqueline Emery, and I am the chief marketing director for Avery. Here and now is the time to ask any auxiliary questions concerning our firm. I will answer the questions you have about Avery to the best of my ability. In about fifteen minutes we will walk the three blocks to our office where you will meet with Amara Chadwick, the owner of the company."

A lady wearing a floral jacket of a mixture of bright colors yelled out, "Is it true that Ms. Chadwick is going to retire? There's a rumor that she has serious health issues."

"She will explain all that to you herself," Jacqueline stated decisively.

"Is Avery still on solid ground financially?" a man spoke slow and deliberately. "I have read that there is some turbulence within the company."

"We have been in business for over forty years, and have never been in better shape financially."

Aaron relaxed in his chair and observed the proceeding. Never once did he have an inkling to ask a question. He was at a disadvantage with the serious candidates for the job, because with all the trouble he was experiencing in his personal life, he failed to do the necessary homework on the firm. He had made himself familiar with some of the advertisement ads created through the company, but beyond that he knew little. The chief marketing director, Jacqueline, was a very good spokeswoman. Her calm demeanor was reassuring, and the more she spoke, the more enamored he became with securing employment.

"When I was approached by the representative from your company, she never specified what positions are available," a young lady stated with a perplexed tone. "Exactly what position am I applying for?"

"All positions are open," answered Jacqueline. "There are going to be major changes at all levels of the firm."

"All levels of the company being open for change is pretty amazing, but I guess we can sort that out through this process," another man asserted pompously. "I do have a good job now. What can Avery offer me?"

"I'll give you some information that each of you might want to take to heart before interacting with Amara Chadwick," Jacqueline stated. "Don't allow Amara's flamboyant appearance trick you. She is a simple woman who believes in the old-fashioned values of honesty, loyalty, and integrity. Character is the most important attribute you can offer to the company, even more important than education, knowledge, and experience. If you do secure employment, you will never find a company that treats their employees better."

"That's a good answer," concluded the man who only a moment earlier asked the question in a manner that seemed as if he was trying to find a way to contradict Jacqueline.

"Now, it is a beautiful day — maybe a little breezy — so you might want to put on a jacket. We are going to walk downtown to our office building."

For the briefest of moments, Aaron wondered why they gathered at the restaurant rather than going directly to the office building. It was a brief thought that he forgot about quickly.

# SEVENTEEN

There wasn't a cloud in the sky as the group walked along the city street. Aaron strolled at the back of the pack. All the interviewees were young and fit, but they needed to hustle to keep up with Jacqueline who was walking at a very fast pace down the wide sidewalk. Several were trying their best to converse with her, but it soon became apparent that it was futile; she was busy leading them to the interview, she had said all she was going to say.

A lady who Aaron had not even noticed at the table earlier kept glancing back at him. She slowed down and soon was walking at his side. She wore a light green crewneck cashmere sweater hugging tightly around her neck, embellishing her beautiful almond-shaped eyes.

"Is there a reason you want to be last in line?" she asked playfully. "Am I missing something about the advantage of being last?"

"Maybe it makes life easier by removing the stress," he said with a chuckle.

"Never thought of it that way. My name is Sofia Balado," she said amicably. Her dark brown eyes were shining, but her right eye twitched a couple of times as she spoke.

"Glad to meet you, Sofia. I'm Aaron Jackson."

"I noticed you were quiet at the meeting."

"So were you," he politely professed.

"I did all my research on Avery before the gathering," she proudly declared. "I'm sensing this is a great opportunity for us. I feel optimistic about the situation."

"I'm hoping for the best." Aaron knew immediately after speaking he was being negative because of the fresh wound he had from breaking up with Sarah. But he felt comfortable speaking with Sofia. Her composure and easygoing manner reminded him of Elizebeth.

In front of them, each person paused and looked off to the right before continuing to hurry down the street. When he and Sofia reached the area where everyone had slowed, Aaron looked over to see what had caught everyone's attention. An old man in tattered clothes, leaning on a makeshift cane made from a piece of two-by-four wood, stood next to an opening between two tall brick buildings. It was too dark to see inside the opening. He and Sofia hesitated, just like the others in front of them, before continuing to proceed forward.

"There's a lady who needs help," the fellow with the cane said in a voice barely loud enough to hear. But Aaron did hear him. "She's stuck in here," the man spoke louder, loud enough to make sure he could be heard.

Aaron stopped and took a deep breath. The man didn't sound very convincing that someone needed help, but he figured it was worth a minute of his time. He walked back to the opening between the buildings. When his eyes adjusted to the darkness, he saw an older lady lying on the concrete against a brick wall, holding her right arm.

"I need some help," the lady said clearly.

Aaron glanced at the group ahead disappearing around the corner of the next block. Sofia followed him back and waited at the edge of the sidewalk.

He leaned into a tight cubby hole. The rancid smell was almost unbearable.

"What in the world are you doing in here?" Aaron asked, staring at the cloud of white hair on the lady. Her body was twisted so she was wedged into the tight area.

"I stepped in here to get a rest," she uttered. "I hit my arm on the edge of the brick. I fell and I can't get up."

"Let me help you out." He reached down and grabbed hold of her right arm and tried to pull. She didn't budge. The smell was awful. He lowered himself to his knees and put his arm under her soft belly and lifted. He pulled her out onto the sidewalk. There was a large smudge on the arm of his tan sport jacket. "Oh my gosh, what is that?"

"I think it's cat shit," the lady said using a matter-of-fact tone, staring him directly in the eyes. Her hands were filthy, and the top of her blouse was twisted, exposing the skin of her right shoulder all the way down to her breast.

"Do we need to call for an ambulance?" asked Sofia, staying an arm's length from Aaron and the soiled lady, covering her nose.

"No, please let me stand and get my bearings. I'll be fine in a moment." The lady stood steady on her feet. She pulled her blouse back in place to cover her shoulder.

"I'll stay here and see if I can get her some help." Aaron looked tensely toward Sofia. "You can go ahead to the interview."

"Are you sure? I can stay with you, too."

"There is no reason for both of us to remain here. I can't go smelling the way I do." He stared at the large stain on the sleeve of his coat. "I'm going to go over to White's Diner and clean up."

"I'll tell Jacqueline what happened." Sofia began walking down the sidewalk, turning to glance back at Aaron, before scampering along.

"Let me look at your arm." He gently tugged on the lady's arm. She winced, but there were no lacerations. "Do you think you can walk to the café? It's about two blocks."

"I know where it's at. I can walk there."

"You can get washed up, and I'll buy you something to eat. What's your name?"

"Abigail," she said meekly.

"I'm Aaron," he stated firmly. "Let's see if we can't get you into a better situation.

# EIGHTEEN

Aaron and Abigail went directly to the restrooms of the café. After washing, he chose a booth at the far back of the restaurant. Duct tape covered some of the cracks of the soft leather of the seat. He pulled his jacket off, folded it with the soiled sleeve toward the inside and laid it on the bench of the booth. There was a large stain on the front of his shirt and when he looked closer, his slacks were also blemished. Looking through a large plate glass window, while waiting for Abigail to come out of the restroom, Aaron watched the people outside walking and mingling on the busy street. There was a tightness in his belly and a lingering thought in his mind, which caused him to realize that he just made a terrible, life-changing mistake in helping the lady. The job at Avery Marketing sounded perfect. Abigail took a long time to clean up in the restroom. When she finally appeared, her hair was damp and combed back. Sliding into the seat across from him, she gave a brief smile before sealing her lips.

"You look much better." He looked closely at her face. Her nose was broad, and her cheeks sagged down from her eyes when she held her mouth shut. When she smiled her teeth were ivory white, and her cheeks would puff out like they were filled with air. Her skin was smooth without any noticeable wrinkles.

She stared at him with clear eyes but didn't say a word. She turned and looked out the window.

"Do you have family I can contact that might be able to help you?" he asked quietly. The smell of the cat excrement was still present. He figured the odor was from himself as much as from her.

The waiter appeared. He stood back from the table, making it very clear that the smell was noticeable.

"I'll have coffee," Aaron said quickly before the waiter could ask for their order. He nodded to Abigail. "Please order something to eat."

"I only want tea, with a dash of milk," she said, queen-like.

"So, is there someone I can call?" he asked again, as the waiter scurried away.

"Nobody." She stared at him as she sat with her back straight. "Thank you for helping me."

Her demeanor was puzzling. There was a quality of dignity, yet he just found her alone, wedged in a culvert. The more he spoke, the tighter her lips became. She sipped her tea in a dainty manner, sometimes holding her pinky finger out, avoiding his questions. It became apparent she was not going to tell him her life story. In fact, the conversation was soon twisted to him. Within a few minutes he was divulging his situation in life.

"Why did you stop to help me when everyone else kept going?" she asked.

"The only answer I can give you is that it was the right thing to do. I believe the other people would have stopped if they had looked closer."

"Where were you going?"

"We were on the final part of an interview for a job with a large company."

"Are you going to lose your job?"

"I never really secured the job, so I guess I didn't have a job to lose," he declared dolefully.

"Is it a job you wanted?"

"Very much so," he avowed. "We were coming from a preliminary interview when I found you in distress. Everything I learned about the company today made me want to work there."

"I'm sorry if I caused you to lose that opportunity." She sipped her tea with a slurp.

"You shouldn't be sorry. I made that decision myself. I am who I am and can't pretend to be otherwise." He smiled and reached across the table and patted her hand. "Having freedom to make my own choices is important to me. Besides, I am good at what I do. I'll find a job."

"Who was the girl that stopped with you?"

"I literally met her five minutes before we came across you," he sighed. "Her name is Sofia."

"She seemed nice."

"I agree," he said cheerfully. "She had a very nice allure about her. I'm sure she would have stayed to help you had either one of us asked her to do so."

"Do you have a girlfriend, or someone special in your life?"

He took a drink of coffee with a gulp. Hesitating for a moment, rubbing his lower lip with the thumb of his left hand before stating woefully, "I did, but we broke up last week."

"I'm terribly sorry," she said with genuine sympathy.

"I want you to know that I don't judge you on your situation." He almost told her that for the grace of God there goes he, but he didn't want to make her feel bad, so he said, "things are not the greatest for me right now either."

"I hope things get better," she said with a deep, sympathetic voice, patting him on his hand.

He stared at her with a bewildered look. A lady he found in the gutter, covered in cat shit, was feeling sorry for him. How far had he fallen.

"Aaron!" someone yelled from a distance. He recognized the voice but couldn't place it.

"Aaron," Charlotte shouted again, moving to the side of the table. Her eyes avoided Abigail. "Sofia told us you left the interview early. I figure you had a good reason."

"I stopped to help this lady," he said, motioning across the table, completely caught off guard by her presence.

"Amara Chadwick's plane was delayed, and she won't be to the office for another hour." Charlotte gave Abigail a half-hearted smile. "You still have a chance for this job, if you want it."

"I don't know." He noticed Charlotte remove a handkerchief from her handbag and put it to her nose. "I guess you can understand why I wouldn't want to interview in the condition I am in."

"There is an executive lounge with a shower back at the office you can use to freshen up," she stated assuredly. "What are you? A medium shirt and 32-34 for pants? I can have them in the office by the time you finish showering."

"That's exactly my measurements," he affirmed before glancing at Abigail.

"You should go," said Abigail. "You were God sent for me."

"There is a shelter not very far from here," he announced with anticipation. "I don't know how long I will be, but if you wait here, I will come back and take you there."

"That won't be necessary. I'm going to be fine." Moisture engulfed the whites of her eyes.

Aaron slid out of the booth. He grabbed his billfold from his back pocket and pulled out all the money from the thin wallet. "Here, let me give you this so you can buy something to eat. It's all I have with me." He handed her forty-four dollars.

She quickly reached out and took the money. Her cheeks puffed out as she smiled.

# NINTEEN

Charlotte, true to her word, had a pair of slacks and a white shirt waiting for him on a chair after he showered in the posh executive bathroom. He combed his hair and stared at his reflection in the steam-covered mirror. His eyes appeared deep and dark with wrinkles resembling crow's feet meandering toward his ears. He heaved a sigh, worried if he was mentally prepared to face the advertising executives.

The conference room was a beautiful reddish-brown color with very expensive mahogany paneling covering the walls, and a large crystal chandelier hung over a long table at the center of the room. There were several drink cups on the table and jackets on the back of cushioned chairs, marking the spot where everyone planned to sit when the owner of the company arrived. The people in the room were all engaged in loud conversation. A very large red chair that looked like a throne was at the front end of the table. There were only three unoccupied chairs at the far end of the table.

Aaron had a terrible, empty feeling. Only a short while ago, he was perplexed as to why he would take the chance of losing a life-changing job to help a stranger, but now he was contemplating running back to help her. He examined the expressions of everyone in the room, and they were all joyous and happy, even after spending hours waiting for the owner to appear.

"It looks like the tortoise is still in the race." Sofia stood very close to him with her hand on the back of a chair. "Was the lady hurt?"

"No, she wasn't hurt badly." Aaron blatantly stared at her. Her right eye twitched twice. The olive-colored skin on her face was pulled tight around her eyes and cheekbones, giving her a natural beauty.

"Why are you looking at me like that?" she asked with a snicker.

"I guess I didn't get a good look at you earlier," he said confidently. "I find you intriguing."

"Wow, that is amazing. We have only said about twenty words to each other, and you have already told me that I am intriguing." She raised her eyebrows. "You can move fast."

"You are intriguing," Aaron said, surprised at how brazen he had become. He scanned her left hand and there was no ring.

"I guess our short time together has been fascinating, and titillating."

"That it has." She was also smart.

"We've been here for quite a while," Sofia indicated using a questioning tone. "I hope they start soon."

"Did you get a chance to speak with the other people here?" Aaron asked. He sensed he should be making more of an effort to mingle with the rest of the interviewees.

"Yes, I did. I don't know if you noticed that everyone is young. After talking with them, they all have a passion for advertising."

Jacqueline, Charlotte, and two other executives from the company entered, and stood at the side of the large table. "Everyone, please take a seat," yelled Jacqueline excitedly. "Amara is in the building and will be here momentarily."

Sofia retrieved her drink from the table nearer the front and moved to the back to sit next to Aaron.

"This ought to be interesting," she stated excitedly, leaning close enough for him to feel her breath on his face. "I have no idea what is about to happen."

"Me neither," said Aaron with a nod.

"I would like to introduce you all to Amara Chadwick, the owner and founder of Avery Marketing," announced Jacqueline, motioning in the direction of a lady walking through the door.

Several of the interviewees clapped politely as a woman wearing a majestic headscarf, but otherwise dressed in a very conservative, yet fashionable, gray business suit, walked to the back side of the large red chair at the head of the table. She patiently scanned the room for several seconds with her hand resting on the side of the chair.

"Hello, everyone!" she suddenly yelled cheerfully, throwing her hands into the air. "It's wonderful to put faces to all of the profiles."

She stopped speaking and took time to look directly at each person at the table. Bright red lipstick enhanced her white teeth as she smiled.

"Yes, if you are wondering, I do have reports and a very good understanding of who each of you are. And I want to say that you are exactly the people we want to move this company forward into the future."

They were finally getting the first glimpse of the celebrated owner of the company. She was obviously confident, flamboyant, and very well-spoken. She spoke rapidly but her words were general without any specific reference to what jobs were open for the group of people.

Aaron looked closer at Amara. Her makeup was perfect. Her fingernails were red, and three diamond rings adorned her right hand. Although he was looking at a very rich woman there was something about her that reminded him of Abigail.

He leaned over and whispered to Sofia, "Does Amara remind you of the lady we just helped?"

Sofia looked for a moment at Amara and shook her head. "Not really," she said weakly.

"Each one of you is being offered a position with the company," Amara happily professed. "We have thoroughly vetted each of you over the past few months, and as I stated before, we are confident you are the people we want to run the company."

Aaron placed his hand on his chin and squinted his eyes to look closer. She had the same broad nose and sagging cheeks under her eyes.

"There has been much speculation over the past year about my wellbeing. I regret to say that those who reported that my health is failing were correct. I have contemplated and discussed with my staff, many of whom have been here since the start of the company, about the future," Amara detailed, using a serious tone. "We have decided to give the company to the younger generation. Every senior member of the organization is supportive of bequeathing the company, and all its holdings, to people who will continue with the mission of creativity through honesty and loyalty, which we established and maintained over the past forty years." She stopped and smiled. "After several months of searching, we have found those people. We have reaped the benefits of this company and now it is time to pass it on."

"That's her," Aaron said. The moment her cheeks puffed up when she smiled, he knew it was her.

"Aaron and Sofia, will you please come forward?" Amara asked, staring directly into Aaron's eyes with a big smile.

He felt lightheaded, as if he were walking on air when he followed Sofia to the front of the room. Aaron stood in awe next to Amara, moving his head back and forth, unsure how to handle the unbelievable change of events. She offered him her right hand. He squeezed the soft hand with both of his.

"How in the world did you get your body to contort into that little space?" he asked good-naturedly, smelling her expensive perfume.

"I practice yoga three times a week." She wrapped her arms around his neck and hugged him tightly. "I wanted to do this earlier."

"You are going to make me cry, but I can't believe you put cat shit in the cubbyhole, too," he whispered in her ear. He felt her chuckle.

"Come here, Sofia." She released the firm grip on him and gave Sofia a hug. When she finished with the embrace, she turned and held up her hand in a royal fashion, motioning to the other interviewees, and said, "I would like to introduce you to the new owners of Avery Marketing."

# TWENTY

Being rich beyond one's wildest imagination takes a while to sink in. Having great fortune fall squarely on your lap is more fulfilling when you come from a station in life where everything you previously touched turned into garbage. The idea that anything in life is possible was now a logical philosophical perception.

Amara was true to her word that she gave her entire company and all the holdings to Sofia and Aaron. A gift worth far more than they could have imagined. The only stipulation was that they hire all the other hopefuls who interviewed for the jobs. Jacqueline was the lone long-term member of the staff to remain in employment. It was also true that Amara was terminally ill. She passed away four months after giving away her company.

It took Aaron nearly six months to convince Sofia to marry him. They were wed in a lavish ceremony at Cherry Hills Country Club and took a two-week vacation to Spain, where he met her aging grandparents. When they returned, they were invigorated and ready to take the company to new heights in the advertising world.

The office where they operated the company was massive with all the newest technological advantages available. By the early 1990's, personal computers were becoming commonplace in many homes. The internet and the networks linked to it were becoming a global system, connecting all parts of the world. It was the beginning of the post war decade with the dissolution of the Soviet Union and the end of Russia as a superpower. America was now the only superpower in the world. Multiculturalism, with alternative music like grunge, and hip-hop was becoming popular. With the new technology the world was changing faster than at any time in history. The advertising industry, like manufacturing and all other businesses, was having to adapt monthly.

Sofia was proving to be insightful in every aspect of the business. She foresaw the digital divide that took place with the new media. The internet afforded both great opportunity and difficulties at the same time. She and Aaron worked well together in solving problems as they figured out how to navigate through the ever-changing world. The company was thriving, the two of them were prospering, and they were very much in love. They made it a tradition to meet with Jacqueline every Friday at four o'clock sharp to have a drink at the Riviera. Arnold continued to be a big part of his life, and quite often, he and Elizebeth would join them at the bar.

The Riviera was a working-person's establishment where they could comfortably discuss all aspects of their lives and simply unwind. Jacqueline was more than a coworker. She was a friend who helped them from the very beginning to understand the intricacies of the marketing and advertising world that could never be understood in the world of academia. She and Aaron had a special kind of connection, where they were on the same wavelength about every decision which came across their desks. And, he was taken with John Henry, Jacqueline's ten-year-old son.

"How was your week?" Arnold asked, sliding next to the wall in a large booth.

"We had a very good week," stated Sofia, holding up her glass of merlot.

"I always look forward to Fridays," Aaron said with a sigh, turning his attention to Jacqueline. "Did you give John Henry the G.I. Joe I found for him?"

"Oh my gosh, Aaron. You are going to spoil that boy to death," said Jacqueline. "He's ten years old now. I would have thought a G.I. Joe was a toy he would have thought himself to be too old for. But he liked it."

"When I saw this G.I. Joe had a scar on its face, I knew I had to buy it. I bet Donnie thought it was cool too."

"Yes, both of them like it." She looked at him and shook her head.

"Action figures and G.I. Joe are popular now. We should try and expand more in that area," said Sofia, speaking over the top of her wineglass.

"With the World War II veterans getting older, the popularity of combat toys might be short lived," stated Elizebeth.

"There are still the Korean War and Vietnam War vets," Aaron stated.

"We should have a statistical analysis on how many World War II vets are still alive and what toys they buy in comparison to the other veterans of war." Sofia tapped a finger on the side of her glass.

"Nostalgia from that generation can be very powerful in marketing." Aaron remembered back to his teaching at the college.

"Good point," said Sofia, noticing apprehension from Jacqueline. "What do you think, Jacqueline?"

"Oh, I agree with everything you said." She took a sip of wine.

"I'm sensing some discomfort with the subject," stated Aaron, using a probing tone.

"My father was a veteran," she specified with an awkward smile.

"I know your father passed, but I never knew he was a vet." Aaron looked sadly at Jacqueline.

"Yes, he fought in the Battle of the Bulge."

"How old were you when he passed?" Sofia asked.

"My mother was pregnant with me when he wrecked his car. So, I never met him." She sipped her wine and looked away, before turning back and saying, "Sorry for being emotional, but it was a very difficult time for my family, especially for my mother.”

“I know you have several brothers and sisters, did your mother raise you all by herself?” Sofia asked.

“I have three brothers and one sister who are older than me and one brother who is six years younger. After our dad’s death, my mother suffered being alone with her children, working hard to support us. We were her whole world, but she soon found that she couldn’t make a living on our farm. We left the country and moved to the little town of Bennett, about thirty miles east of Denver. Every summer the town would be filled with harvesters who came to cut the wheat. Mom fell in love with a wheat harvester and married him. That is where my little brother came from,” Jacqueline stated.

“Your mother is still alive, isn’t she?” Aaron stared at the slits of Jacqueline’s eyes and her protruding forehead. Although she was only six years older than him, he noticed some gray poking out of her hair.

“Oh yes, she still lives in Bennett.”

“Your mother sounds like a very strong woman,” proclaimed Elizebeth admiringly.

“I would really like to meet her,” Aaron abruptly stated. “She sounds like an amazing woman. What’s her name?”

“Betty. I think she would appreciate meeting you too.” Jacqueline gave him a slight smile.

They sat quietly for a moment drinking their wine before Aaron turned to Jacqueline.

"Thanks for sharing that and thank God it's Friday."

# TWENTY-ONE

By 1996 the world continued changing with the World Wide Web growing quickly. Improvements in products such as digital video discs, Palm Pilots, and mobile phones were changing the American culture. Marketing firms scrambled to keep up with the new technology.

Many couples found that working together was a kiss of death for their marriage. For Aaron and Sofia, it was just the opposite. With time, their love for each other became stronger. On September 15, 1996, Sofia gave birth to a beautiful little girl named Carmella Jean. Life changed forever for the two of them. Taking leave from a life of promotional blitzes, sweeping media campaigns and anticipated product launches, they now looked forward to spending time with the baby.

Delegating the ability to make executive decisions to the different departments within the company soon became ordinary business. Everything went like clockwork for five years. But by 2001, with the change of the century, the fast-moving world caught up with the old ways being implemented by Avery Marketing. For the first time the company was facing financial difficulties. Both Sofia and Aaron realized they needed to concentrate on the company.

Carmella was a spitting image of her mother with smooth brown skin and beautiful almond eyes. Her spirit was animated with a buoyant disposition. It was decided that she would be homeschooled and accompany her parents to the office rather than attend kindergarten. Jacqueline was slowly becoming tired of the hustle and bustle of the business but was still one hundred percent supportive of Aaron and Sofia. Rather than meeting at a bar for Friday afternoon decompression they would meet at McDonald's for ice cream and time with Carmella.

Jacqueline, more times than not, would pass on playtime at McDonald's because of John Henry's high school sports schedule. But this particular Friday night, she made it a point to meet Sofia, Aaron, and Carmella after work.

"One of us is going to have to go to New York City next month to meet with the software people," stated Sofia immediately after sitting down at a booth across from Jacqueline and Aaron near the play area of McDonald's. Carmella sat quietly next to her.

"I'll go," said Aaron. "Many things are back on track with the company, but we still have a lot of disagreement internally about the techniques we should focus on in promoting products. It is essential we find consensus among everyone so we can continue to work as a team."

"Is there something bothering you?" Sofia gently asked, noticing Jacqueline staring off blankly.

"I know this is a terrible time to do this, but I am going to have to take some time off. At least a month."

"Of course. We will support you with anything you have to do." Aaron sensed that it was a very trying time for Jacqueline. "Is there any way we can help you?"

"I don't think so," she said with a sigh. Heavy, dark bags hung under her eyes. "My mother is going to have surgery, and I want to be with her."

"I hope it's not serious," said Sofia.

"It's for her knee. I think it will be ok. She is going to stay with me next week so she can be close to the doctor's office for pre-surgery consultation. And then after the surgery she will be at my house for rehabilitation."

"Your mom's name is Betty, isn't it?" Aaron asked.

"Yes, it is. Good memory."

"Your mother has been on my mind ever since you shared her story with us," said Aaron. "I would still like to meet her sometime."

"She will be at my house on Monday," Jacqueline said with a more joyful tone. "Why don't you all come over for dinner Monday night? John Henry would love to see you."

"Are you good with dinner Monday night at the Emery's?" Aaron asked Sofia.

"Sure, we haven't seen Donnie or John Henry for quite some time," said Sofia.

"It's a date," confirmed Jacqueline. "I should get going so I can make it to John Henry's football game. It's more of a scrimmage, but I still want to be there."

"Where are they playing tonight?"

"Colorado Springs. I have plenty of time to get there if I leave now."

Aaron felt a sense of loss as he watched Jacqueline leave the restaurant. He was glad she wanted to take time off for herself, she worked hard her entire life. She was very wealthy and deserved to find happiness. But he was pretty sure this was the beginning of the end of her time with the company.

# TWENTY-TWO

Aaron walked up the steps of Jacqueline's home in the upper-class neighborhood in the suburban town of Parker. Sofia, holding Carmella's hand, strolled right behind him. Sitting on the front porch was an old bicycle with a wooden handlebar.

"Look at this old bike," Aaron said with excitement, running his hand across the smooth oak handlebar. "It must be more than a hundred years old."

Donnie greeted them at the front door. He was a sophisticated, wealthy man who tried hard to seem ordinary. He wore a blue T-shirt with *Newport* written across the chest.

"Come on in," he said, opening the door wide. "Everyone is in the family room."

"Whose bike is this?" Aaron asked.

"Oh, that is the bicycle Jacqueline's father rode on when he first met Betty," Donnie stated. "They are giving it to John Henry."

"Well, it is just awesome," declared Aaron.

It was always uncomfortable greeting Donnie. Aaron wasn't sure if he should shake his hand, and Sofia felt like she should give him a quick hug, but he always turned and left them standing. They followed him to the family room.

Jacqueline was sitting on the sofa next to her mother with John Henry on the opposite side of them looking at a scrapbook. John Henry immediately rose from the couch and came to greet Aaron. He was about six feet tall with giant biceps and a massive chest.

"How are you guys doing?" He put out his hand and shook Aaron's hand vigorously.

"Good Lord, John Henry," Aaron said with a smile. "How in the world did you get so big?"

"My gosh, you've changed." Sofia leaned in and put her right arm around his neck for a quick hug.

"Come here, Carmella." He bent down and picked her up. She began to giggle. "You think I'm big, look how big she has gotten!"

"Come on in," said Jacqueline. "I want you to meet my mother, Betty."

"It is a pleasure to meet you," said Sofia, reaching down and gently shaking her hand.

"You have the most beautiful eyes," said Betty.

"Thank you, my father calls them Spanish eyes."

"And your daughter was blessed with them too," said Betty, staring at Carmella in the arms of her grandson. "She is a little darling."

"And this is Aaron," declared Jacqueline.

Aaron stared at the freckles on Betty's cheeks and her brownish-gray hair.

"Glad to meet you, Aaron."

"It's truly my pleasure," he said. "I understand you are going to have surgery on your knee."

"Seventy-eight years of wear and tear finally caught up with me," Betty asserted with a chuckle.

"Mom was a professional roller skater when she was young," stated Jacqueline. "She also worked at Remington Arms carrying around heavy boxes of shells during World War II, and I'm sure that didn't help either."

Aaron felt a great sense of déjà vu. Being a great student of history, he often felt as though he experienced a situation before. Betty was the personification of many women from the 1940's and 1950's.

"You are a real-live Rosie the Riveter," he declared.

Betty kept her head steady and moved her eyes to look at him. "That I am."

"Dinner is ready," yelled Donnie.

"Mom made us an angel food cake with chocolate fudge frosting for dessert," said Jacqueline proudly.

Aaron found it hard to concentrate during dinner. The story of Jacqueline's family tragedy and the strength of her mother was inspiring. The angel food cake was the best dessert he had ever eaten, but he wanted to get dinner over so he could learn more about Betty. He wished he could figure out a way to package her inspirational tale of grit and determination into a thirty second commercial.

After dinner, Betty felt comfortable with speaking freely about her life story. The scrapbook she brought was full of pictures about her time with her husband Henry, but also with pictures that told a story about life after his death. Aaron found it mesmerizing to sit on the couch, shoulder to shoulder, with the older lady studying the photos.

"Your red hair was really beautiful."

"Thank you. Now, this is a picture of the old house we moved into when we left the farm," said Betty, holding a picture of a small house with faded white siding.

"Looks pretty small for you and five kids," Aaron said.

"There were only two bedrooms, and during the winter the snow would blow into the bedroom from the uncaulked areas around the windows."

"It must have been a very tough time for you trying to make ends meet after your husband's death," interjected Sofia.

"I would be lying if I claimed those times were anything but difficult," stated Betty.

"Did you have a job?" asked Sofia. She sat in a chair while John Henry and Carmella played with a Tickle Me Elmo on the carpet in front of her.

"I sold Minnesota Woolens door-to-door and worked part-time as a waitress for the local truck stop. Between those jobs, I would make cinnamon rolls and pies for the café." She picked up a picture of a little girl standing in a field next to a man. "Here's a picture of Jacqueline right after running in a race at the harvest festival. I think she was about eight or nine."

"Who is she standing next to?" Aaron asked.

"That was her stepfather, Jack. He was a custom wheat harvester I married about seven years after Henry's death. He is the father of my youngest son, Michael. Jack passed about eight years ago."

"So, you have had two great loves in your life," stated Sofia.

"I appreciate you framing my life in that way, Sofia," Betty said, looking at Sofia in a favorable manner. "I never liked it when people felt sorry for me. I have been so lucky in my life."

"I find it inspiring for you to have such a positive attitude after facing so much adversity," declared Sofia.

"Adversity and challenges have kept my life dynamic. The hardship and difficulties our family faced created a great and wonderful bond, forged in love with one another."

"Who's this?" Aaron pointed at a picture of Betty and another woman standing next to the front doors of a large building.

"That's my best friend, Pearl. She and I were in New York City in front of the World Trade Center." She paused for a moment. "We were there fifteen years ago, in 1986."

"That's an awesome picture," Aaron enthused. "I am going to be at the World Trade Center for business next month."

"The weather should be nice in September," Betty replied.

"Everyone in New York was good with changing the meeting from later in the week to Tuesday so Aaron can be back to celebrate Carmella's birthday on Saturday," Sofia declared.

"I saw the itinerary," said Jacqueline, sitting down on the couch next to her mother, on the opposite side of Aaron. "You're arriving in New York City on Monday, September 10 and meeting at the Trade Center on the 11th and 12th then flying back on Thursday the 13th."

"Doesn't sound like much time for sightseeing," Betty stated with a smile, looking into Aaron's eyes.

"I'll be honest." He glanced at Carmella still playing on the carpet with John Henry. "I would rather be here with Carmella to celebrate her birthday week."

"Oh, the things we do for the business. Would anyone like a glass of wine?" Jacqueline asked. "I know you wouldn't, mother."

"I have never had alcohol touch my lips, and I never will," Betty avowed with a determined tone.

"That is amazing. I'll pass on the wine," Aaron said. He thought about mentioning that it was even more incredible to go through a life of losing two husbands and raising six children without some sort of liquid support, but he held his tongue. "How about you Sofia? You don't have to drive."

"I'll pass, too," she said graciously.

"Here are some of Henry's pictures from his time in the service. He dated each entry, along with the locations." Betty's hand shook as she held a small notebook. "I found the book and pictures in his sock drawer after his death. He never told me a thing about his time overseas. I really wish I had pressed him more on the subject. People always regret things when someone is gone."

"Can I look at it?" Aaron asked.

"Absolutely," she handed him the notebook.

Aaron carefully thumbed through each page of the fragile book. History was his favorite subject in college, especially stories about the depression years and World War II. Holding the chronicle from a soldier during that period was inspirational. He imagined the emotions Henry must have experienced while fighting in Europe. He sat, in a catatonic state, staring at the book.

Sofia noticed that Betty's shoulders were relaxed and her eyes stayed fixed to Aaron's face as he looked at the book. She was watching him with an expression of serenity as though they were connected by an unknown component.

"Thank you for sharing that with me," Aaron said respectfully, handing the notebook back to Betty. "It would be interesting to have a professor at one of the colleges look at this book."

"I think I will leave that up to John Henry." Betty looked at her grandson sitting on the floor. She yawned. "He can decide how much he wants to learn about his grandfather."

"Did you have a lot of support from people after the death of Henry?" Sofia asked.

"People, many who I had never met before, gave us support and comfort. But it was my family who really came to our aid." Betty's tone was one of approval for the question from Sofia. "The first year was the most difficult and it was the time where I received the most assistance. I realized that eventually I would have to step up and take responsibility for caring for my children, which I did."

"Every one of us went to college," chimed in Jacqueline.

Aaron noticed Betty yawn again. "We should head for home. We have a very long drive."

"Yep, we should," said Sofia agreeably. "It's already past Carmella's bedtime."

Sofia sat in the back seat with Carmella, who fell asleep immediately after they began the drive home. A bright moon shined a light on the highway, with very little traffic, making the drive home one that allowed Aaron's mind to wander. He now had a better understanding of Jacqueline and her family. Theirs wasn't a story

of defeat and pity, but one of happiness and
strength.

# TWENTY-THREE

Aaron and Sofia were aware of the reason for Avery Marketing being in a slump, and they both agreed on how to remedy the situation. Many clients were not happy with the financial results, verified by data, for the promotion of their products by the company. It wasn't the communication techniques, or the delivering and exchanging of offerings, that was afoul, it was the creation of them. Over the past year, shock and awe, along with surprise stunts, were used to promote products while ignoring important things to a customer such as value, availability, and quality of service.

A week before Aaron's planned trip to New York City to try and resolve the issue, he and Sofia left work early to take Carmella to the Denver Zoo. The weather could not have been more ideal. They walked along the sidewalk, stopping to view the different animals with Carmella in between holding their hands.

"I wonder if we shouldn't delegate someone to go to New York City." Sofia's right eye twitched several times, unsure why she brought up the subject at that time.

"No, I need to speak with everyone face-to-face." He had not noticed her eye twitch in quite some time. "This is too important to delegate."

"I hate to see you miss time with Carmella before her birthday."

"I plan to spend so much time with my little girl that she will be asking me to go away."

"I doubt that," Sofia chuckled.

"Can we get ice cream?" Carmella asked when she saw the refreshment booth.

"Of course we can," affirmed Aaron. The bright sun was radiating off the sidewalk. "Do you want me to carry you?"

"Yes please." Carmella reached her arms up high and placed them around her dad's neck. She squeezed as hard as she could.

"Wow, that is the hardest hug I have ever seen," Sofia said, watching the two of them continue to hug as they walked in the direction of the concession stand. The feeling in her belly was one of pure bliss, seeing her daughter and husband so happy.

"Let's take a break here on the bench and eat our ice cream," said Aaron, sitting on a metal bench.

"You know what we are going to see?" Sofia wiped a chunk of ice cream off Carmella's chin. "A lion."

"I don't want to see a lion," Carmella said, pushing her dirty face into the side of her mother.

Aaron took the small bowl of ice cream out of Carmella's hand. The hot sun turned the ice cream into a small bowl of liquid mush. A lady with gray hair and large glasses sat on a bench with her husband blatantly staring at them. The lady noticed Aaron looking back at her. She rose up and limped in their direction with a big smile on her face.

"These are times you should cherish," the lady stated, using a soft and pleasant tone. "Your daughter is adorable. We used to bring our children here when they were younger. I want to tell you that these are the experiences in life that you will treasure. Take your time to enjoy them because they are fleeting."

"Thank you, Ma'am," said Aaron. After spending the evening with Jacqueline and hearing her mother's story, the caring gesture from the woman resonated well with him.

"Yes, thank you," echoed Sofia.

"You're welcome," the lady said before limping back to her husband. They slowly walked away.

Aaron leaned back and watched Carmella crawl into Sofia's arms where she hugged her mother. How fortunate could one man be he thought. His life had become unimaginably fulfilled.

"Come on, Carmella." He placed his hand on her shoulder and rubbed while she continued to cuddle on Sofia's lap. "Let's go look at the lions. If you want, I can hold you."

Carmella stood up on the bench and then jumped into his arms. They walked to the lion's den.

"Do you see the lion?" Aaron held his daughter as they watched two large lions prance back and forth. "Look how beautiful they are."

"They are not scary at all, are they?" Sofia said lightheartedly.

"No," said Carmella.

"It's hot out here." Aaron placed his hand on Carmella's forehead. "Maybe we should head for home."

"No, let's stay a little longer. I want to see the camel," Sofia stated adamantly. She placed her hand on his bicep as he continued to hold their daughter. "It might be quite a while before we get back here."

"All right, let's go see the camels," conceded Aaron, feigning enthusiasm. He took a quick step away from the lion den. They walked toward the camel exhibit.

"Are camels scary?" Carmella asked.

"Yes, they are terribly scary," he said, squeezing her tight. "But mommy is a camel fighter and will protect us from them."

"No, they are not scary. In fact, they are nice," said Sofia with a smile.

"Look how tall it is," said Aaron.

"How tall is it?" Carmella asked.

"It's this tall." He lifted her as high as he could.

Sofia leaned back and watched the two of them interact. A great peaceful feeling flowed through her body.

"I think we should head for home," said Aaron. "Someone here is getting tired."

"I'm not tired." Carmella laid her head on his shoulder.

"You know what I think?" Sofia asked. "I think we should get a pet."

"I want a kitten," yelled Carmella.

"Who's going to take care of it?" Aaron dipped his head to stare at Sofia.

"You are, of course."

"Daddy is."

"We'll talk about this when I get home from New York."

A kitten would be a nice addition to the family. He and Sofia never officially stated that Carmella would be their only child. It was more an unspoken understanding that when it came to children, they were one and done.

## TWENTY-FOUR

Aaron woke early the morning of September 9th with the idea that he and Sofia would work the entire day in their home office, streamlining ideas for a new ad for suntan lotion. Suntan lotion was the product they decided to use in their presentation, illustrating to the personnel within their own company their vision of how to improve relationships with clients without the use of provocative or taboo imagery to sell their products.

Carmella played on the floor in the office while her parents worked. By midafternoon, they felt confident that they had perfected the demonstration, and that Aaron could present the message in an effectual manner to the executives of the company.

"Carmella, come up here and let's practice typing on the computer." Sofia twisted in the office chair to allow her daughter to hop on her lap.

Carmella placed her fingers on the keyboard without any coaching from her mom.

"Move your right finger to the J," whispered Sofia in her ear. "Ok, now your left finger to the F."

Aaron watched them cuddle as they practiced typing the alphabet. He moved his gaze to the walls of the large, perfectly decorated office where a picture of cubes and cones hung on the paneled wall, an original Pablo Picasso painting. It was only fifteen years earlier that he had stared at putrid wallpaper peeling from the wall of his decaying apartment.

"What are you thinking?" Sofia gently asked, gazing at him with her beautiful eyes looking over the top of Carmella's head.

"I'm thinking how unbelievably lucky I am. I have a beautiful wife, a beautiful child, and more money than I could spend in my lifetime."

"We are fortunate." She swung around on the office chair, holding Carmella tightly around her waist.

"We should give more back," stated Aaron philosophically. "Create a charity."

"What charity are you thinking of creating?" Sofia asked with a puzzled tone. "I'm totally good with giving back, but we should do it in a manner that has a positive outcome for those we want to help."

"I don't know, I only know it would be right for us to do so now," Aaron sighed. "We can look into it further when I get back from New York City."

"Are you packed?"

"I need to get the suitcase from the basement." He rose from his chair. "But first, I think I should give someone a ride."

He picked Carmella up and placed her on his shoulders. She placed her hands on the top of his head while he held her legs tight with his arms. He ran around the room.

"Watch her head," yelled Sofia as they exited the office.

They ran down the hallway past the bedrooms and into the kitchen. When they came back into the living room, Aaron was limping slightly. He lifted Carmella over his shoulders and onto the carpet before sitting down and rubbing the side of his leg.

"Did you just hurt your ankle?" Sofia asked with a perplexed tone.

"Not really. I just need to rub this cramp out and it will be ok." He massaged the side of his foot a moment longer before rising from the floor. He took a couple steps. "It's fine," he said with a smile. "I'll grab the suitcase out of the basement."

Aaron's ankle gave way on the first step going down into the basement. He tumbled all the way to the bottom of the steps where he grabbed his ankle and screamed. Sofia wasted no time in calling for an ambulance.

Aaron's ankle was fractured. He was still in great pain when they returned home from the hospital, but was able to hobble into their house using crutches and stepping gingerly on the walking cast. It was obvious he could not make the trip to New York only a day and a half away.

Sofia called the office and had them make the arrangements for her to take his place.

Aaron called Arnold to see if he and Elizebeth could come stay at their house for a couple days while Sofia was in New York City. The Broncos were playing Monday Night Football, and it would be special to spend that time with his old friend.

## TWENTY-FIVE

Aaron was woken by the sound of his cell phone ringing. He glanced at the alarm clock — it was four-thirty. He realized immediately that it was six-thirty in New York City, and Sofia was calling right before she made her way to the World Trade Center.

"Good morning," he answered cheerfully.

"Well good morning. You sound like you were already awake."

"I'm faking it," he chuckled. "I was in a dead sleep. Arnold and I stayed up late and talked after watching the Bronco game."

"How's your ankle?"

"Sore, but I'll live," he said dismissively. "Are you ready for the presentation?"

"As ready as I'm going to be."

"I wish I was there with you. The more I thought about it yesterday after you left, I wished I would have gone with you."

"That's why I love you," Sofia said tenderly. "It's better you are there with Carmella instead of limping around here. Everything here is in fast motion."

"I know you will handle it brilliantly."

"I need to get going," Sofia said. "The company car is supposed to be at the front door of the hotel right at seven. I just wanted to talk with you before I go."

"Have you eaten?"

"I'll pick up a pastry and coffee there."

"Make sure to call me when you get a break."

"The first meeting is scheduled at 8:30 with the graphics people," she said anxiously. "I need to get going so I'll call you from the office. Love you."

"Love you, too."

Aaron's ankle was throbbing. It took all the strength he could muster to climb out of bed and, using the crutches, limp into his closet to get dressed.

It was six-thirty by the time he sat down at the kitchen table with a pot of coffee brewing. He leaned over and placed his head on the table and grimaced. The pain in his ankle was excruciating. Elizebeth walked into the kitchen wearing a light blue terrycloth bath robe.

"Are you alright?" she asked.

"I should have taken it slower getting out here," he sighed. "It will take a moment for the pain pill to kick in."

"What's going on, buddy?" Arnold stepped into the kitchen wearing baggy pajamas with pictures of purple kittens.

"Ankle is a little sore this morning."

"Why don't you sit in your recliner and turn on the news?" Arnold suggested. "Elizebeth and I can cook up some eggs and bring breakfast to you."

"That was a big win by the Broncos last night," stated Aaron, taking hold of his crutches. "I really appreciate you two staying here until Sofia returns."

"It's nice that we can get together," said Arnold. "Your home is very comfortable."

"What time does Carmella usually wake up?" Elizebeth asked.

"If I don't wake her, she will sleep past eight."

"I'll have her breakfast ready at eight. If she's not up, I'll wake her."

Aaron sat down in his chair and raised his legs up off the floor. He stared at the television — an expensive 55-inch plasma flat screen that he had mounted above the mantle on his stone fireplace. Placing the tv remote and his cell phone on a coffee table next to the chair, he felt a twinge of concern for Sofia, realizing that she should be well into the meeting. He saw on the clock that it was nearly seven o'clock; nine o'clock in New York. He turned on the television so he could catch the start of the morning news.

A banner for a special news alert flowed across the bottom of the screen showing that an airplane had crashed into the World Trade Center. He leaned forward in the chair and lowered his feet. It seemed surreal as he stared at the screen.

"Arnold!" he yelled, stepping out of his chair and leaning on his crutches.

"What's going on?" Arnold asked anxiously.

"Something has happened at the Trade Center. I need to try and call Sofia." He dialed on his phone. It went immediately to a lost signal; he stopped the call and tried again.

"Do you know which tower Sofia is in?" Arnold asked.

"It's the North Tower," stated Aaron nervously.

Elizebeth stepped into the room and stared at the television. Another airplane crashed into the side of the South Tower. "Oh my God," she yelled, placing her hand over her mouth.

All three stared at the television in utter disbelief.

"There are a lot of firemen going in there," Arnold said anxiously.

Aaron tried calling Sofia on his phone. Still no signal.

"Try calling your business office," said Arnold.

Aaron dialed the business office.

"Hello, Avery Marketing," the voice was very pleasant.

"This is Aaron Jackson; I need to speak with the supervisor."

"Mr. Jackson, I'll transfer you to Mr. White."

"Aaron," said Mr. White in a weak voice.

"Marvin, do you have any specifics on what is happening in New York?"

"I can't tell you anything in detail, because right now I don't know," he stated firmly. "I do know that it doesn't look good. Our people are on the upper floors of the North Tower."

"Call me the moment you have information," demanded Aaron. He felt a terrible throbbing in his head.

"Oh my God, it just collapsed," yelled Arnold. "It just imploded."

They watched on the television while a large plume of dust rolled across the streets below. The defense mechanisms within his mind wouldn't allow him to believe that Sofia was caught in the nightmare taking place before him. He thought of every possibility that would have taken her away from the meeting at the top of the North Tower.

"That was the South Tower that just fell," stated Arnold sadly. The skin on his face was sagging so much that the redness in the lower part of his eyes was visible.

Aaron dialed Sofia's telephone number. Still no connection.

"I hear Carmella moving around in her room," said Elizebeth exhaustedly, "I'll go in and sit with her."

Arnold moved next to Aaron, who was staring at the television in a catatonic state.

"Aaron, I wish there was something I could do to make this easier for you," Arnold said sadly. "All this mayhem doesn't seem real."

Aaron continued to stare at the television without saying a word.

"I have never felt so helpless." Aaron sighed. He could hear the muffled voice of

Carmella speaking with Elizebeth in the back bedroom.

Arnold wanted to tell his friend to remain positive, instead he stood close enough for his shoulder to brush Aaron's arm. They watched silently as the North Tower crumbled to the ground with a cloud of dust rushing outward.

Aaron continued for the next hour to look forward as if he were looking past the television. His phone rang.

"Hello," he answered hopefully. "Yes, Jacqueline..."

Arnold was close enough he could hear the conversation through the phone. It was a hard blow to take. Everyone was still holding hope of a miracle, but Jacqueline was unable to reach anyone in the New York office. They ended the conversation with the idea she would call as soon as she heard anything definite about the fate of the Avery team.

"Daddy." Carmella stood behind him staring at the television.

"Come here honey." He picked her up into his arms. She continued to stare at the television. He clicked the television off and hugged her tightly.

# TWENTY-SIX

The world changed. Making sense of hatred was not a component of Aaron's disposition, so he didn't even try to add it to his process of grieving. Never could he have anticipated a life where he would experience such a sharp transformation from happiness to sadness. The fall from glee to grief cut much deeper into his being than did the rise to riches he experienced earlier in life. His spirit was crushed, and his soul was cast down. He fell so deep into the darkness that he questioned if he wanted to continue to live.

Again, at a time of need, he used Arnold and Elizebeth as his crutch, the difference now was he had Carmella, and her well-being was the most important aspect of his life. Aaron fancied himself as a people person, who understood much about the behavior of the masses. With the sadness, anger, and fear everyone was feeling, television ratings for the news covering the horrific attack were at an all-time high. Human nature was such that people couldn't stop watching something that brought them dread and anxiety. For him, it was difficult to find any glimmer of goodness in a turbulent sea of misery.

Over the following months and years, Aaron learned one important lesson: life goes on. While his mind was in a cloud of confusion, life was happening. Carmella was growing quickly, and before he realized it his little girl was graduating from middle school and going into high school. It had been nine years since the passing of Sofia.

The first time he saw Martha Mathews was when he went to the school orientation for Carmella's ninth grade class. She was a beautiful Chinese lady with jet black, shoulder length hair, dressed in a light gray pantsuit. She stood out in an auditorium full of parents. Even from a distance he could tell she was classy and refined. It was she who initiated the first contact with him.

As she approached, he made eye contact with her before she spoke, "You must be Carmella's father," Martha proclaimed confidently, obviously knowing he was.

"Yes, I am." He stared a little too long at her pretty face without asking her name.

"I'm Polly's aunt, Martha. I've heard so much about you all," she declared with an exaggerated Southern accent. "Ever since I read about the loss of your wife Sofia, I have said many prayers for you."

"Ok. Uh, thank you for the prayers." He could see a necklace with a silver cross hanging on her neck. He never heard Carmella mention anyone named Polly, but he didn't want to embarrass the beautiful aunt of a girl who was potentially going to be a friend of his daughter at the new school. A thought came to his mind that her praying for him was a ploy to scam him out of money.

"I was wondering if you might be free to have coffee tomorrow morning?"

What in the world? He had just met her, and she was already asking him out. Now, skepticism of her intentions filled his thoughts. He stared at her without answering.

"I apologize for being so forward, but I am only in town until tomorrow evening." She could see the uncertainty in his face. "I own a car dealership in the Dallas area and would like to speak with you about some marketing ideas."

He glanced across the large open auditorium at the other parents mingling. He felt an awkwardness with the situation with Martha, but he chalked it up to having been away from female companionship for so long. She certainly intrigued him.

"Sure, why not," Aaron spoke with a confident tone. "I know of a quiet coffee shop very close to here where we can meet."

"Perfect." She placed her hand on his bicep.

***

Arnold rubbed his chin as he sat in his easy chair while Aaron leaned back on the sofa across from him. Both men held a glass of Jamison on ice in their hand. Elizebeth worked on dinner in the kitchen alone, something that concerned Aaron about the health of his friend, because over the years Arnold was the one who considered himself as the chef of the family.

"So, this lady just walked right up to you and introduced herself?" Arnold struggled to take a breath before continuing. "So, just out of the blue she came into your life?"

"Is that so unusual?" Aaron asked, using a tone of perplexity.

"Yes, it is. Is she attractive?" Arnold leaned in the direction of Aaron and looked him directly in the eyes.

"Yeah, well..." A large smile came across Aaron's face, "yes, she is very attractive."

"Ha, just what I thought. Believe me, she knows everything there is to know about you," Arnold stated firmly, laboring with his breathing. "You need to take this all very slow, because she will eat you up and spit you out."

"All we're doing is having coffee — nothing else."

"That's not taking it slow. This 'nothing else' is going to turn into a lot more."

"Give him a break, Arnold," yelled Elizebeth from the kitchen.

"Thank you, Elizebeth," yelled Aaron in her direction.

"I know women, believe me, I know women really well," whispered Arnold. "A rich, somewhat good-looking guy like you, can be a sitting duck for a pretty woman. She wants far more than you can see. You have the resources to have her checked out. That's all I'm requesting here, have her assessed before getting too involved."

"You know I'm not completely naïve," declared Aaron.

"Yeah, but you have been out of the game for a long time," Arnold assessed.

"What game would that be, Arnold?" yelled Elizebeth from the kitchen.

"I think he's talking about the game of laying around and watching television all day," Aaron shouted toward the kitchen with a chuckle.

"Ha, ha," Elizebeth snickered loudly.

"Very funny. I just want you to be careful." Arnold leaned back in his chair, knowing that he had gotten his point across.

"You know I will be. Thanks for the advice."

Arnold had put on quite a few pounds over the past year and was looking incredibly old. His skin was still smooth but dark bags hung below his eyes and his hair had thinned to the point of him becoming completely bald. Aaron was concerned about the health of his lifelong friend. But even with the physical deterioration, his penchant for analyzing and identifying troubles in the world was as strong as ever, his mind was very sharp. He knew that everything his friend mentioned had a ring of truth to it.

# TWENTY-SEVEN

Martha was waiting for him at a table near the back of the large 1950s-themed coffee shop. A large picture of Marilyn Monroe hung on the wall above her. There was a long line of people lingering to order coffee, so he decided to forgo purchasing a beverage. Martha stood up and put out a hand for him to shake as he approached the table. He took a seat across from her. They were isolated with all tables around them empty, something that made him feel comfortable, as if he were trying to hide a secret.

"I am so happy you decided to meet me this morning," Martha announced quite loudly. Her euphoric demeanor was ever apparent in every gesture she made. A twenty-ounce paper cup of coffee sat on the table. "I wasn't totally positive you would show up."

"You were very forward in your approach to me yesterday," stated Aaron, noticing the top two buttons of her blouse were undone, and that there was a faint smell of whiskey in the air. "I guess you piqued my interest."

"Our meeting this morning could end up being very beneficial for both of us."

"You mentioned that you own a car dealership in the Dallas area." He felt uneasy with the situation. The circumstances of her wanting to meet him so unexpectedly felt convoluted.

"Actually, I own one-half of the dealership," she emphatically stated. "The other half of the ownership wants out of our partnership."

"Are you wanting me to buy them out?" Aaron asked with a distraught tone.

"In one word, yes."

"Now what would make you think that I am interested in owning half a car dealership in Dallas, Texas? I find it insulting that you would tell me that you were interested in marketing ideas and then try to coax me into buying part of your dealership."

"Ok, ok. Allow me to explain." She could tell he was angry and about to leave. She took a large gulp from her coffee cup and leaned across the table. "My partner and I have been having trouble with the dealership for over a year. He wants out, but I know with the right business practices, the dealership is a gold mine. I researched marketing companies to hire, and Avery Marketing is at the top. While investigating the company, your profile came up. I thought with your marketing skills, the opportunity for you to own part of the company might be something you would embrace. But my initial intentions were to hire a marketing firm."

"Coming to such a conclusion is beyond brazen of you," Aaron contended angrily, and quite loudly. "This is a ridiculous situation you are putting me in."

She closed her eyes and shook her head, knowing that her technique and abruptness in offering him part of her business was becoming a total disaster.

"I am so, so sorry I brought all this up in such a hasty manner." She leaned over the table and placed her right hand over the top of his left hand. "I'm usually not anywhere near this bold."

"I'm sorry you are having such a hard time with your business." He sensed her vulnerability and eased his scorn.

"I apologize again for throwing all of this in your lap in such an awkward manner without any explanation." She stood up. "The line has disappeared for coffee, allow me to get you a cup and we can start all over again."

"First, I have something to ask you." He hesitated for a moment while she waited over him. "Do you have booze in your coffee?"

"About half full of Irish crème," she candidly answered. "How would you like yours?"

"Just black."

As Martha walked away, he closed his eyes and took a deep breath. The thought of leaving the situation entered his mind. Something in his soul told him he should at least wait and hear her out. But, if she talked him into buying the dealership, and he was scammed in any way, shape or manner, Arnold would never let him live it down. His mind was spinning when she arrived back with the coffee.

"Hi, my name is Martha Luan Mathews, and I just bought you a cup of coffee," she declared lightheartedly. She placed the cup of coffee in front of him and took her seat across the table. She intensely stared at him through her pulsating dark eyes with her bright red lips closed tightly.

"Do you have any more Irish Crème?" Aaron inquired in a businesslike manner.

She reached into her briefcase. He walked to the trash can and emptied half of the coffee into the trash receptacle. She refilled his cup with the liquor. After taking a big swig, his shoulders went limp, and he let out a deep breath. He could see the bare skin at the top of her chest, along with the gold necklace and cross she wore. He felt a bit lightheaded. It took him a moment to gather his thoughts before he spoke. "Our world is full of advice and guidance," he wearily stated. He could feel the liquor flow through his blood stream. "Almost always this counseling comes with little thought or effort from the person giving the advice. It's a strange human condition people have that makes them feel better when they help others. Don't you agree?"

"I agree," she quickly replied. She would have agreed with him even if he told her Marilyn Monroe had just come alive and was standing behind her.

"Every person in my life would recommend I get up right now and leave our meeting." He raised his hand to point at the picture of

Marilyn Monroe. "Look at Marilyn Monroe up there, why are we remembering her decades after she passed?"

"I really don't know," she awkwardly answered, wondering if he might have some serious mental problem that was unnoticed during the screening process she paid for.

"Why would you come here and ask me to bail you out of your financial mess?" Aaron brought his attention back to her. "I really want to know the answer to that question."

"I am literally at my wits end trying to find a buyer that will work with me so I can keep the dealership I have worked my entire life to build," she sighed.

"Out of all the people in the world, I am your last option?"

"Best option, not last," she candidly answered.

"Alright Martha Mathews, how much money are we talking?"

"Somewhere around eight million," she quickly responded.

"Do you have a niece in Carmella's class?" he inquired.

"I have a niece in Carmella's school, but she is a year older."

"You do know that I will check out every nook and cranny of this business before I give you a cent." He looked her directly in the eyes. "My accountants are very good, and there is no way you can trick me out of my money. This will have to be very beneficial to me."

"It is not a scam." She sniffled. "This business has been my whole life."

"Did you inherit it?"

"Oh my gosh, no. I built every bit of it from the bottom up," she proudly declared.

"Who's your partner?"

"Ex-husband number one," she stated dolefully.

"So, you had more than one husband?"

"Yes, but I was smart enough to have a prenuptial with number two, so he has nothing to do with the business."

"And number one is good with selling?"

"He very much wants out. The great recession really hit his real estate holdings hard, and he needs the money in the worst way."

"You don't have the ability to buy him out?"

"The recession hit me hard too," she confessed. "I have tried to find a way to buy his share, but I can't." Her breathing became much deeper as she stated, "this is really a good opportunity."

"So, you have been married twice, with both ending in divorce?"

"Actually, three times. The third one was very brief and ended with an annulment."

"Are you trying to lure me into marrying you, or is this just a business deal?"

"Just business. You are way too nice of a guy for me to entice into marriage," she declared.

It was fortifying to have an acute faith in your position in life that no matter which way the wind blew any decision you made couldn't be wrong. Aaron was free to make choices with the realization that if they were initially wrong, he was surrounded by those who would make corrections. He felt deep in his soul that he should take the deal.

"Ok, Martha, I want you to send me all the financials and proposals for the business."

She stared at the gray hair on the sides of his head with a big smile on her face. He had just saved her.

Little did she realize, giving her hope was remarkably restorative to his own being. He lost his zest for life after Sofia's death. He was now ready to live again.

**TWENTY-EIGHT**

Two weeks after Aaron became a partner with Martha in the Dallas car dealership, Arnold sat down on his recliner in front of the television and fell asleep. He never woke up. It was only fitting he should die in such a peaceful manner. For Aaron, losing a lifelong friend, who he leaned on during times of crisis, was terribly troubling. It created a sense of urgency within his own being that his time was limited.

Owning half of Martha's car dealership was beyond fruitful; it was exciting and thriving. She was correct that all the business needed to succeed was some thoughtful advertising. She was a perfect business partner who allowed him to independently make marketing decisions, while she continued to run the everyday aspects of the dealership using her knowledge and experience. Both were content with keeping their relationship businesslike and nothing romantic ever developed.

Well after the age when most people retired, Aaron realized the fast-paced life of dealing with the intricacies of both the car dealership and Avery Marketing was becoming exhausting. He retired and found that spending time at home working on improvements to his large backyard was extremely fulfilling. The aches and pains of growing old were something he tolerated with an attitude of understanding that it was all better than the alternative. Aaron could feel, deep in his bones, that his living days were nearing an end, but held a great sense of serenity in the realization he had lived a full life. For the first time, he found time to read. Such books as *The Count of Monte Cristo* and *Pillars of the Earth* helped him be cognizant of the fact that humans had always suffered and endured.

It was as if he blinked and all those closest to him had passed. Carmella and John Henry were the only two people left that he considered to be close. John Henry relocated to New York City, so he was rarely seen. Sofia was very busy with work but would stop by to enjoy an afternoon with her father watching the squirrels and birds play in the backyard. But for the most part he spent time alone, some days not even speaking a word to another living soul.

One day, while staring at a large dirt berm off to the side of the patio in his backyard, he envisioned a beautiful stone retaining wall, with three oak trees behind it. So, he hired a stonemason to build the wall. He was fascinated with watching the mason work. He recalled the first time he met Sofia, and she asked him if there was an advantage in being last. He told her that it made life easier by removing stress. He was now able to live that stress-free life. There was something spiritual in watching the old man meticulously cut each stone and place it on the wall. The mason made a point of stopping after work every day to talk with him about subjects ranging from sports and politics to life's lessons in general.

It was a beautiful September day when the mason completed his work. Aaron sat on the patio with a cup of lemonade on the table in front of him. His white hair was tousled and a ten-day-old making of a silver beard covered his jawline and chin; a sign of liberation for a man who had religiously shaved the first thing every morning for most of his life. He watched as the builder finished cleaning the stone cap of the Colorado buff strip stone wall.

The mason approached with a paper statement in one hand and a bottle of water in the other. He had a full head of gray hair and was slumped over as he walked to the table with a slight limp.

"Mr. Jackson, do you mind if I sit and enjoy your backyard with you for a moment or two?" inquired the mason, handing Aaron the invoice for his work.

"Certainly, you can. Would you like a glass of lemonade?" Aaron placed the bill on the table in front of him.

"No thank you, sir. I just want to rest a moment before I finish gathering up my tools and head home." His clothes were noticeably wet as he sat in the cushioned chair across the table from Aaron. He placed his bottle of water in front of him. "I sure have enjoyed working here. I hate to see the job end."

"I can't tell you how much I appreciate your work."

"I've been doing this for a long time — my whole life." With all the faux stone, it has become very hard to find a job where I can build using natural stone. Fake stone is cheaper and doesn't require a qualified mason to install the material."

"I certainly appreciate your creativity and time you took with the smallest of details to make such a beautiful wall. The extra expense of using natural stone was well worth the cost."

"I appreciate that," the mason replied with a smile, staring at the deep lines from the wrinkles on Aaron's face. "Can I ask you a personal question sir?"

"Certainly."

"How old are you?"

"I'm eighty-six years old." Aaron answered. "My body feels every year of it, but my spirit is still young."

"I always tell those who watch me limp around that aging is living," the mason professed.

"I know time is very valuable for a man who works for himself. Sometimes when you took the time from working to talk with me, I felt as though you were my guardian angel," revealed Aaron with a very soft voice.

"I wish I would have spent more time chatting with you. The older I get, I find that by the end of the day all I want to do is go home and sit in my easy chair."

"Well, I enjoyed watching you build the wall. I found it fascinating that you cut every single stone using a hammer and chisel."

"Some stonemasons use a saw with a diamond blade. I guess I'm old-fashioned," confessed the mason. "I notice you have the book *Pillars of the Earth* on the table. It is one of my favorite books. I use some of the same tools now as they did with stonework back then."

"I never thought about that. A lot has changed since the 12th century, but a lot hasn't."

"That certainly is true. I guess both me and Tom Builder have something inside our souls that drive us to try to build something consequential," said the mason.

"I imagine that is the type of characteristic that allowed you to stay in business for so long," evoked Aaron.

"I heard you talking with the landscapers about the placement of three small sapling oak trees on the berm behind the stone wall. You made it clear to them that the trees should be placed where they can eventually give the maximum amount of shade for the patio," he stated.

"Yes, they plan to plant them tomorrow."

"It'll take several decades before a sapling oak tree will give shade. That tells me an awful lot about what kind of man you are." He stood up. "Now, if you don't mind writing me a check, I need to get going home."

***

As Aaron lay on the hospital bed, taking his final breaths, Carmella sat at his side, holding his hand. The hospice nurse stepped to the side of the bed. All life saving devices were turned off.

For the entirety of his life, he never had the clarity he held right before dying. He thought about all he experienced, relishing each thought. "I had a good life," he proclaimed. "I wish I could do it all over again knowing what I know now, but death is the toll all of us must pay at the end of the road."

"Are you afraid, Dad?"

"No, not of dying," he sighed. "I'm sad because I'm leaving you, and sad because I won't be able to see what happens next in the world." He squeezed her hand as his breathing became shallower. "I believe that death is just the next step. I believe this very strongly."

"I'm glad you believe in the afterlife so passionately. I hope I can have the same belief when it is my time to go," she declared in a timid voice, realizing he was struggling to speak. "You don't have to speak if you don't want to Dad."

There was a great amount of contentment in his soul from sitting with his beautiful daughter, who was now a brilliant and accomplished woman. Both realized it would be the final time for them to be together on earth. There was silent agreement to appreciate the moment, unlike any instance they experienced together before.

"I can't believe that with so much love and laughter in the world that it will all end when we die," Aaron struggled to make the statement, hoping to ease the pain between the two of them, allowing that they would be together again.

"I never told anyone this before: when I came out to look at the television as you watched the Twin Towers fall, I saw angels in the dust," her voice became softer. She could tell her father had lost the strength to speak but could tell by his expression that he was happy to hear her confession.

Aaron thought back to that moment when he was holding her in the living room right after the towers fell and she couldn't keep her eyes off the television. He was unsure what she might have seen as a child, but he hoped with all his heart that it truly was an angel she witnessed in the dust. But he was too weak to tell her.

"I'll miss you terribly, Dad." She leaned in and kissed him on his cheek.

The last thing he felt was the soft hand of his daughter squeezing his wrist.

# TWENTY-NINE

A blinding white light triggered Aaron to slam his eyes shut. When he opened them, he was sitting on a bench in front of a crystal-clear river running through a park of bright green lawns and trees. The sky was perfect Cerulean blue. An old lady sat close by him with her arms crossed. Sitting next to the lady was a young woman with short black hair and a small button nose.

"Just take a deep breath," the old lady commanded with a deep, gruff, gravelly voice.

He relaxed when he heard the wind blowing through the trees.

"You seem to know where you are," the younger lady cited with a very thick British accent.

"It's pretty obvious that I am dead."

"Yes, you are, but very seldom do we see someone so content. Most seem quite twitchy," the young woman lamented, glancing in the direction of the older lady. She received a very stern look in return.

"I feel confident that I have lived a positive and principled life. I sensed that when I reached the Pearly Gates, I would be embraced with open arms."

"This place hasn't been called the Pearly Gates for quite some time," the older lady replied.

"Is this area heaven, or is there more?" Aaron sensed he had been at the precise location before, but his memory was a little foggy.

"A lot more," the older lady stated before clearing her throat.

"There is so much more," the younger lady gushed, flinging her arms out to her side. "It's all just unimaginable. I have followed your progress for eons, and I am completely and utterly chuffed to be a part of your journey."

The older lady placed a hand in front of her and motioned downward, signaling to the younger woman that she should tone down her remarks.

"What do you mean by my progress?"

"You have been marvelous in your past lives," she cooed, "and when you sorted out the chap who was harassing Betty without the least thought of fear…"

"Alright, stop right there," yelled the older lady with a raspy voice. "You have crossed way over the line of our authority. That kind of a statement could cause him to plunge into a complete state of confusion."

"I'm trying to bring him calmness and blessedness. You know complimenting someone isn't that bad of a thing."

"Aaron." An image in the far distance appeared.

"Sofia?"

"Yes, we'll talk soon." The image disappeared.

"Ok, let's move on. Can you hand me the piece of paper in your shirt pocket?" the older lady requested with a voice that seemed to originate from deep in her chest."

"My mind is still foggy about all of this, but I realize that I have been here before." He could see the bright green trees moving in the breeze and the tall building in the distance rising into the clouds. He turned to the younger woman and asked, "who are you?"

"She is someone I am training," the older lady answered quickly.

"I'm just learning," stated the younger woman.

"How did you end up here?" Aaron asked.

"You will have to ask all your questions to others. That is beyond our pay grade. I can tell you that everything we do here is very structured. There is no guessing," the older lady proclaimed.

"What is your role?"

"Simply to bring clarity and blessedness to help you move to the next level."

"I have followed your stories for quite some time," the younger woman enthusiastically confessed. "I find you to be such a wonderful person with an abundance of moral clarity."

"Hold your tongue!" yelled the older lady.

"The moral courage you have shown in your lives is just delightful. And, oh my gosh, the love you have found." She gave Aaron a big smile and batted her eyes.

"What are you doing?" asked the older lady incredulously. She held her mouth wide open while staring at her trainee. "You do know you are not helping him."

"So, you're not supposed to answer questions?" Aaron inquired.

"We can answer basic questions, but not the ones about your life, or this process."

"What happens if you do? Are you going to find yourself shoveling dirt out of a ditch, instead of greeting people?"

"I guess, something like that," she proclaimed with a gruffy voice, still gawking at her trainee.

"On earth as it is in heaven is pretty accurate than," stated Aaron. "I remember much more of this now."

"Uh huh. Let's leave it there and get going before this situation gets us all in trouble," she stated hoarsely, clearing her throat again. "I have a lot of work to do with this trainee."

He felt a great sense of comfort when he entered the room with the walls of bright, pastel colors. The door with light radiating around it was just as he remembered, and the enrapturing lady behind the glass desk brought him contentment.

"Well, you lived a full life. Have a seat," the lady greeted him enthusiastically. She motioned in the direction of a padded leather chair to the side of her desk.

"Although I lived what is considered a full life, I still have questions," he professed.

"Questions are good. Go ahead and ask."

"Why is there so much chaos and contention on earth? Is the world about to end?"

"There always has been instability, confusion, and turmoil. Humanity always finds a way to adapt and overcome the bedlam."

"It seems the more we advance, the more problems we create."

"The bigger the problem, the more fulfilling the solution."

"You don't seem at all worried about humanity. Why not?"

"There is more compassion and love, and understanding on earth now than I have ever witnessed before. It is just being overlooked."

"But why does there need to be so much wickedness?"

"Do you feel you are immoral or evil?"

"No, not really. I could have been a better person. But I would never consider myself to be immoral, and certainly not evil."

"Everyone needs grace. Humans are imperfect. All people have the capacity to be immoral, but most choose to be virtuous and ethical, just like you. The bad on earth is being highlighted, while the good is ignored."

"The world I came from seems like it is more than just flawed, it seems there is evil."

"Of course, there is evil. Think of all the people you interacted with; weren't most of them kind and compassionate?"

"I lost the one person I loved the most through an act of malice, how can that be good?"

"The prospect of losing someone creates love. Loss has a way of reminding people what matters. Even the thought can deepen love. If the chance of losing a person you love isn't reality, then the idea doesn't work. As I said before, there is far more kindness and compassion on Earth than there is evil. Malevolence by a few doesn't mean all of humanity is wicked." She spoke with a calm voice. "Do you have any more questions?"

"Why don't you give everyone the answers to make the world perfect?"

"There are an infinite number of answers beyond human comprehension. It is why I only answer specific questions."

"I feel like I wasted most of my life," he confessed.

"Most humans do."

"What is humanity's purpose, why do we exist? There must be a purpose."

"Ha, most people ask why I exist, not why everyone exists. Your purpose is different from others, and it is part of the puzzle for humanity. It is important for people to want to live, grow, experience all that is offered and to create. But the best single answer I can give for why humanity exists; it would be to make the world a better place."

"As I prepare to go back, it makes perfect sense to me now. I think I understand."

"I'm glad you feel that way, but you really do not. We haven't even scratched the surface of it all."

"I want my name to be Jerome when I return to earth."

"Ok, Jerome it is. Now, go meet your angels."

He made his way through the doors with the bright lights. The sense of angels coalescing with the people from his long past was so powerful that it caused him to close his eyes to let it all sink in before continuing inside. He remembered how people on earth tried to define what they thought heaven would be. He now agreed with those who proclaimed, "heaven is so beautiful that it is undefinable."

THE END

OR BEGINNING

# ABOUT THE AUTHOR

Dan Peavler grew up on the eastern plains of Colorado where he graduated from Bennett High School. He played on the Metropolitan State College of Denver's basketball team from 1970 until 1973. He graduated from the University of Colorado with a Bachelor of Arts degree in Psychology in 1975. He and his family moved to Littleton, Colorado in 1989. He volunteered hundreds of hours as a youth sports coach and spent five years as a basketball coach with the Littleton High School girls' basketball program. Having worked in construction with his own masonry company and experienced the excitement of the ups and downs of the real estate market as a real estate broker, while enjoying the elation of being a part-time author, he has found nothing more fulfilling in life than spending time with his exceptionally large family.

# Dan's Other Books

**2051** - The War on American Soil trilogy chronicles the terrifying concept of Americans fighting Americans as foreign enemies invade the homeland.


**The Toastmaster** - A captivating story of the triumphs and struggles of ordinary people. It is a story of love, loyalty, and survival.

# Reading Group Questions

1. What was the most surprising moment in the entire novella?

2. What theme resonated most: destiny, free will, suffering, or love?

3. What was the most emotional scene for you?

4. What do you think the author is saying by showing three different lifetimes connected by the same soul?

5. Do you agree with the afterlife guide's explanation that suffering is tied to human choice, not divine design?

6. If you could change one event in the story, what would it be?

7. What do you think the "levels" and "floors" symbolize?

8. Do you think the story portrays humanity as mostly good, mostly flawed, or something in between?

9. Have you ever had an instant connection with someone?

10. What single word best describes the novella's message?